# Joyce Cary

# *Joyce Cary*

# THE DEVELOPING STYLE

### *by JACK WOLKENFELD*

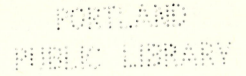

1968

NEW YORK
New York University Press

LONDON
University of London Press Limited

# Acknowledgments

I have tried to annotate my debts to the many critics who have written about Cary. I am glad to acknowledge a special debt, however, to Andrew Wright, Hazard Adams, and M. M. Mahood whose outstanding studies of Cary have given me far more than acknowledgment can indicate.

My thanks must also go to Dean Hyman Lichtenstein of Hofstra University and Ruth Miller of the University of the State of New York at Stony Brook, who long ago laid the foundations for this work; to John Unterecker, William York Tindall, and Robert Gorham Davis who read the manuscript and made valuable suggestions for its improvement; and to John O. H. Stigall who gave the support of a mentor, colleague, and friend.

Acknowledgment is made to Harper and Row, Publishers and to Michael Joseph Limited, for permission to reprint excerpts from *Not Honour More* (1955), and *The Captive and the Free* (1959).

Acknowledgment is made to Harper and Row, Publishers, Michael Joseph Limited, and Curtis Brown Limited, for permission to reprint excerpts from the following books by Joyce Cary:

*The African Witch,* Copyright 1936 by Joyce Lunel Cary; *The Horse's Mouth,* Copyright 1944 by Joyce Cary, reprinted by permission of Harper and Row, Publishers; *Aissa Saved* (1962); *An American Visitor* (1961); *Castle Corner* (1963); *A Fearful Joy* (1949); *Herself Surprised* (1941); *Mister Johnson* (1951); *The Moonlight* (1946); *Prisoner of Grace* (1952); *To Be a Pilgrim* (1942); *Spring Song and Other Stories* (1960).

Acknowledgment is made to Harper and Row, Publishers and Cambridge University Press for permission to reprint excerpts from *Art and Reality* (1958), by Joyce Cary; to University of Texas Press and Martin Secker & Warburg Ltd., for permission to reprint excerpts from *The Case for African Freedom and Other Writings* (1962); to the University of Washington Press and Ivor Nicholson & Watson Ltd., for permission to reprint excerpts from *Power in Men* (1963).

Excerpts from "Political and Personal Morality," by Joyce Cary are reprinted by permission of *Saturday Review;* excerpts from the Joyce Cary Interview originally published by *The Paris Review,* issue no. 7, are reprinted by permission of *The Paris Review* and The Viking Press, publishers of *Writers at Work: The Paris Review Interviews* (series 1), and Martin Secker & Warburg Ltd.

Excerpts from M. M. Mahood's *Joyce Cary's Africa* (1965), are reprinted by permission of Houghton Mifflin Company, and Methuen & Co. Ltd. Excerpts from Isaiah Berlin's *The Hedgehog and the Fox,* Copyright 1953 by Simon and Schuster, Inc., are reprinted by permission of Simon and Schuster, and Weidenfeld and Nicolson, Limited. Excerpts from Andrew Wright's *Joyce Cary: A Preface to His Novels* (1958) published by Harper and Row, are reprinted by permission of the publisher. Excerpts from *Comedy,* edited by Wylie Sypher (1956), are reprinted by permission of Doubleday and Company, Inc.

Permission to reprint brief excerpts has also been granted by *The Cornhill Magazine, Harper's Magazine, Inc., The Listener* (The British Broadcasting Company and Curtis Brown), *The Nation,* Princeton University Press, *PMLA,* University of Pennsylvania Press, and *Vogue.*

# Contents

# Introduction

Joyce Cary stands aside from the major grouping of contemporary novelists, a lone figure who created his own work in his own way. Certainly he does not seem close to those writers who are most specifically associated with the twentieth century, and who helped to mold the modern novel as something emphatically different from the fiction of the past. The main effect of these writers—James Joyce, Joseph Conrad, Virginia Woolf, to name only a few of those writing in English—was to develop a new form for the novel. They experimented with a variety of stylistic devices to create dense, heavily textured works which would stand alone as shaped objects. Although they certainly had a great deal to say to modern man, they appeared far more like priests performing a divine service than like prophets delivering a divine message. In contrast to their works, Cary's novels have none of this experimental appearance, none of this essential concern with stylistic matters. They have what seems rather an old-fashioned characteristic of emphasizing the story as a series of events which occurs to characters of memorable vitality. On the other hand, Cary's novels do not seem to fit into another important contemporary kind of fiction, the kind which seeks to use literature as one of the tools with which to effect changes in society. If Cary is a didactic novelist it is not because he wants to teach his readers what to do but only because he wants his readers to learn what reality is like.

Cary's career itself has an unusual look. Though he thought of himself as a writer very early in his life, his first novel was not published until he was forty-four years old, retired from one profession, and had taken another ten years or so reading and studying in order to develop his own view of things. Cary spent his early years as a young artist, poet, university student, and adventurer. In 1913, Cary settled into the African Service where he fought in a world war and then administered an enormous territory, virtually on his own. He seemed well on his way, during these years, to becoming an African expert, one of the sort he described in the character of Jim Latter in his second trilogy, upright, nonintellectual, with a number of inflexible rules—a man who is always a few years out of date. Nonetheless, he wrote a great deal while in Africa, though the manuscripts were all unsatisfactory because, he said later on, "They raised political and religious problems I could not answer." [1] Leaving the African Service, in 1920, he settled down to his major task in Oxford, and it was not until 1932 that he had his philosophy worked out enough to produce his first publishable novel.[2]

When briefly glanced at in this way, Cary seems to stress the statement of his work out of all proportion and to ignore the form which makes any statement possible in a work of art. A more intense look at the works themselves, however, reveals a very close relationship between the two elements of art. They are indeed so organically interconnected that it is impossible to disentangle, even if one should want to do so, what Cary's novels say from the way in which they say it. This is also how Cary himself thought of the matter. "The form of a book . . . ," he said, "is not in some artificial pattern, some formula, but in its relation to ultimate truth." [3]

It seems to me that this is fundamentally true about all works of art, and that it points to the right way to approach Cary. One reason, for instance, why Cary moved so naturally toward the multiple novel is that he saw reality as made up of a number of fragments. His use of the multiple point of view corresponds to his conviction that an individual can only grasp one portion of that reality. The interlocking of the segments grasped by the various points of view, on the other hand, corresponds to an equally strong conviction that there is a single objective reality. The frantic quality of the narration, similarly, fits into Cary's view that the social situation is by its nature dynamic, always changing as a result of inevitable conflict.

Such an approach indicates, to me at least, that Cary's lone position among contemporary novelists comes not so much because he is not modern as a writer or a thinker, but rather because his vision required another way. It would have been extremely inappropriate for him, for instance, to write in the way of Conrad, with whom Cary has been frequently compared.[4] Conrad's typical works produce a sense of wholeness, as is most obviously seen in *Heart of Darkness,* a novel in which the plot and the thematic development are almost entirely a movement into the center, first of the Congo, then of his statement, and finally of the empty heart of darkness. In Conrad as always the symbol unifies, and since Cary needs to show multiplicity he cannot write symbolist novels.[5]

It is for such reason that I am out of sympathy with attempts to place Cary among the eighteenth- and nineteenth-century novelists—Defoe, Fielding, Dickens, and Trollope, for instance—because they, like Cary, did not write with a modern concern for form. In any event, since most of the novelists after the thirties, especially in England, were just as unmodern as Cary, though not in exactly the same way, I do not find the judgment to be one which distinguishes Cary's quality.

Mark Schorer may be somewhat more helpful when he says that Cary wrote "socially extensive" novels, by which he means novels which aim "to encompass the quantity and only secondarily the quality of social experience," and which do not have a fundamental moral concern.[6] This view, too, is not mine, however, since the implied denigration in such a placement strikes me as being quite aside from the main point.

This study, therefore, is an attempt not to place Cary but to define him, by looking both at the general consistency of his work and at the development within the generally consistent pattern. In order to do so I examine both Cary's manner and his matter.

## Notes

1 John Burrows and Alex Hamilton, "The Art of Fiction VII: Joyce Cary," *Paris Review*, No. 7 (Fall-Winter, 1954–1955), 74.

2 For an outline of Cary's biography, see Andrew Wright, *Joyce Cary: A Preface to his Novels* (New York; Harpers, 1959), Chapter One, pp. 13–27.

3 Joyce Cary, "The Way A Novel Gets Written," *Harper's Magazine*, CC (February, 1950), 92.

4 See, for instance, M. M. Mahood, *Joyce Cary's Africa* (Boston: Houghton Mifflin, 1965), p. 146; Wright, pp. 26, 73; and Warren G. French, "Joyce Cary's American Rover Girl," *Texas Studies in Literature and Language*, II (1960), 290. French goes so far as to say that the case of Marie Hasluck pushes beyond that of Kurtz in *Heart of Darkness*. Conrad showed only the destruction of a "superficial idealist," French says, while Cary showed the shortcomings of a "conscientious idealist."

There is, of course, no question that Cary was influenced by Conrad, as he made clear a number of times, for instance, in the *Paris Review* interview, p. 72. Specific echoes of Conrad in Cary's work can be noticed in the characterization of Bewsher, who is very much like Lord Jim, and of Chester Nimmo, with his great voice and his final loneliness, is very much like Kurtz. Note also the insistent sea imagery in Cary, pointed out by George Garrett, "The Major Poetry of Joyce Cary," *Modern Fiction Studies*, IX (1963), 245–56.

5 William York Tindall in *The Literary Symbol* (New York: Columbia University Press, 1955), p. 16, says: "For author and reader the symbol is unitive."

6 Mark Schorer, "The 'Socially Extensive' Novel," *Adam International Review*, XVIII, Nos. 212–13 (November-December, 1950), 31.

In an approach very much like Schorer's, a great many of Cary's critics agree that Cary's outstanding characteristic is his simple vitality, his unprogrammatic mimesis of real life, and they either praise or blame Cary for it according to their personal bias. Their leading member is Robert Bloom, who wrote a book-length attack on what he calls Cary's "moral indeterminacy." See Robert Bloom, *The Indeterminate World: A Study of the Novels of Joyce Cary* (Philadelphia: University of Pennsylvania Press, 1962). On the other side of the argument, M. M. Mahood makes a convincing case for her view that at least the African novels are, if anything, too thesis ridden.

# Abbreviations

All references to Cary's novels are to the Carfax edition published in London by Michael Joseph, except for the following two novels: *Except the Lord* (London: Michael Joseph, 1953) and *The Captive and the Free* (New York: Harpers, 1959).

The page references follow citation in the text and are in parentheses, with the following abbreviations identifying the individual works:

AS: *Aissa Saved*
Am V: *An American Visitor*
Af W: *The African Witch*
CC: *Castle Corner*
Mr J: *Mister Johnson*
Charley: *Charley Is My Darling*
H of C: *A House of Children*
HS: *Herself Surprised*
TBP: *To Be a Pilgrim*
HM: *The Horse's Mouth*
Moonlight: *The Moonlight*
FJ: *A Fearful Joy*
P of G: *Prisoner of Grace*
ETL: *Except the Lord*
NHM: *Not Honor More*
C and F: *The Captive and the Free*

# Joyce Cary

# 1. Juxtapositions and Confrontations

*The African Witch,* Joyce Cary's third published novel,[1] opens with "an awkward incident"—the intrusion of two uninvited Africans into an area normally reserved for whites and their carefully selected guests:

> It is usual, for convenience, to reserve the paddock for invited guests, and in practice this arrangement excludes all the natives except a few magnates like the Emir and his Ministers.
>
> The Emir of Rimi has never attended the races, but he is always represented. On this occasion, three of his chief officers—dignified persons in blue and white robes, wearing large blue turbans—took up their places at one side of the enclosure, near the starting-post, before the first race, and remained there conversing among themselves for the rest of the day. They were an ornament to the occasion.
>
> But when, just after the first race, the European spectators, turning away from the ropes, saw two negroes in European dress, one a very tall mulatto, one darker and shorter, strolling across the private ground, they felt strong surprise. This became indignation when it was known that the intruders had not been asked (15 *Af W*).

Besides describing the intrusion, this opening serves a number of important purposes. It introduces the basic situation of the novel, which deals with the unsuccessful attempt of

Louis Aladai, one of the two offending Negroes, to assume the native political control of Rimi. The opening may even be considered as a kind of embodiment of the total novel, with several of the details accurately forecasting events. For instance, Aladai's struggle is primarily with the native power structure, the Emir and his court, but since this power is under the protection of the British administration, his struggle for the emirate becomes inevitably entangled with British policy. The clothing of the Africans is functional too, since what they wear indicates the degree of their Westernization. The acceptable Negroes thus are an ornament in their native costumes, while Aladai and his colleague are offensive in their Western clothes. In *The African Witch*, as in Cary's other African novels, the whites prefer for various reasons not to see Africans dressed in Western clothes, or to speak English, or to have adopted Western culture, and they use the term "trousered ape" to describe the Westernized African.[2]

The violence which in this case is aroused in the whites is another significant element of the book. One of the Europeans says, "They ought to be put down and beaten. That's the only way to teach such brutes!" (15 *Af W*). And later the very man called on to do the beating, Captain Rackham, actually does physically hit Aladai and precipitates one of the crises in the book. Calls for violence come also, repeatedly, from Aladai's companion in the paddock, the Reverend Selah Coker, and these calls, too, are fulfilled by events.

That the occasion of the opening is a horse race is largely part of an ironic thrust at the British, who frequently play games while political events of primary importance go on around them. This is most clearly seen when the British community is busy developing their newest game, bagatelle, while events are leading to the death of the local missionary and a British girl, as well as to a serious revolution (277–87 *Af W*). Ignorant of the true affairs in the area they are supposed to be administering, the British do, in fact, seem to be playing a game all along, especially since most of them have much less at stake than most of the Africans.

The opening pages of *The African Witch*, then, show

Cary consciously concerned with his craft and carefully arranging his material for formal effect. In this functional prefiguring of the novel in the introduction, Cary is like a great many other novelists.

There is something else in this opening, however, which is more individually typical of Cary himself, and it can be noted in both the image and the language of the quoted paragraphs, which place heavy stress on the opposed ideas of exclusion and invasion. Thus the paddock is "reserved," natives are "excluded," the ground is "private," the two Africans are "intruders." The image itself shows an area physically set off for a special group in the process of being literally invaded by two men who do not belong to the group.[3]

A glance at some of Cary's other early works will indicate just how often he sends his main characters into territory closed off from them by tradition or by law. *Aissa Saved,* the first of Cary's novels to be published, has as its main framework two repeated invasions of a pagan stronghold by a group of Christian natives, against the orders of the British district officer, against the counsel of the missionary, and against the dictates of common sense. In *An American Visitor,* Cary's second published novel, the story develops around the attempt by a group of miners to enter the land of the Birri; they are opposed by Monkey Bewsher, a district officer who hopes to close off the land against them and other similar representatives of Western culture. In *Castle Corner,* published next after *The African Witch,* members of various social groups try to enter into territory belonging to another. In the first chapter, for instance, an Irish family has barricaded its hut against the landlord, John Corner, while the clearest example of the theme occurs when one of the Corner cousins, Harry Jarvis, with a detachment of soldiers invades a previously closed off province, Laka, and "conquers" it for England (160–75 *CC*).

What is generally considered Cary's finest African novel, *Mister Johnson,*[4] also centers around an invasion, though in this case the invader is an inanimate object, a road which intrudes into the previously static area, Fada, and which allows newcomers to intrude as well. Furthermore, Mr. Johnson himself is intruding into a tribal area where he is a stranger.

In *The African Witch,* the invasion in the opening scene is followed by a number of others and is complemented by a number of parallel evasions, imprisonments, and escapes—all of them functioning to show the relationship between the various political and personal forces which operate in the work. As a matter of fact, the plot of the entire book is structured on these achieved or avoided confrontations, revealing in this way the actual situation in Rimi.

Aladai, the only Rimi native to have received a Western education, considers himself the heir of the present emir who is eighty years old, and he demands support for his candidacy in opposition to Salé, a young Moslem who has the backing of many in the palace group. In Aladai's camp at the opening of the book are three principal supporters: first, there is his uncle Makurdi, a businessman who has sponsored Aladai's education and who "knew better than anyone in the country what could be done with Rimi and Rimi trade by an intelligent Emir guided by a businessman of his experience" (26 *Af W*); then there is Coker, a native fundamentalist Christian preacher; finally there is Elizabeth, Aladai's half sister and the priestess of the local ju-ju cult.

These last two, though both supporters of Aladai, are opposed to each other both in religion and in fundamental approach to life. Ironically enough, it is the Christian, Coker, who is irrational, with a sacrificial urge which demands that blood be spilled—his own as well as that of others. The pagan priestess, on the other hand, is essentially rational and practical in her approach to both politics and religion.[5] Aladai, though caught in the middle, opposes both the uncivilized, retrogressive ju-ju of Elizabeth and the violent bloodthirst of Coker. His precise relation to each becomes clear through his invasions of their strongholds.

His opposition to Elizabeth is relatively clear-cut and it is shown clearly by his invasion of her ju-ju house along with the missionary, Dr. Schlemm, in order to rescue a girl who has been accused of witchcraft (137–38 *Af W*).

On the other hand, Aladai's relation to Coker is much more ambiguous. Aladai does invade Coker's camp—characteristically Coker preaches his mixed version of Christianity in an abandoned ju-ju grove, a place where he can more easily summon the violence of the primitive which he seeks for his bloody religious needs—and he and his people do rescue Judy Coote, who had once been his teacher at Oxford (263–64 *Af W*). Nonetheless, he is never in full opposition to Coker and he is never seen as really invading Coker's camp. Indeed, he seems to belong there as much as not. Perhaps this is the very reason that when the story line requires a fight between the Coker and the Aladai parties, the fight is not presented, but only reported in the third person: "What happened in Rimi the rest of that morning is not exactly known. . . . But it was heard through the political agent Audu and the Resident that the man Coker had quarrelled with Aladai and attacked his party. . . ." (218 *Af W*).

This ambiguous relationship comes to a climax in a scene which shows Coker's triumphant religious meeting. Aladai at this meeting is a clearly divided figure, on one level caught by the power of Coker's call for blood and sacrifice, on the other making logical comments about it: "He swayed, and the moans tore him like giant hiccoughs; he couldn't stop them. But his brain was working" (292 *Af W*). Echoing Coker he moans, "We all must die. . . . He that is first—must be the sacrifice." But he adds immediately afterwards, "I shall speak to Miss Judy about this. Why this lust for death? It does not seem natural" (292 *Af W*).[6] In fact, Aladai's relation to Coker is as much that of prisoner as of invader.

Aladai's opposition to the Mohammedan claimant to the emirate, Salé, is unambiguously clear and his invasion of the town, in company with Judy Coote, leads directly to a battle in which he becomes heroically victorious (49–55 *Af W*). A clear-cut confrontation with the Emir's forces never occurs, however, even though the invasion of the town is in a sense in opposition to the Emir because the Emir is actually not a force any longer to be contended with; he is too old and feeble to have a real effect. Insofar as he makes any real effort, it is to avoid confrontation. Thus he banishes, in vain as it turns out, both contenders for the succession, Aladai and Salé. His people, the Master of the Horse, and the Waziri, for instance—interesting examples of powerful individuals lost in the structure of a feudal court—similarly have no real power and are not shown as either directly invading or evading.

Another group not shown in conflict with any other is that surrounding Musa, the youngster who leads his followers into a no-man's-land between the pagan and the Mohammedan parts of town. The fact that he is in a no-man's-land is significant and it places him in a position of freedom in the sense that he is in the margin between two worlds without belonging to either. He is in fact personally also a free character, a leader by strength of his personality. His role in the book, however, is to exist as a mimic, a mocker of all parties, and thus to cast ironic light on all of them. By virtue of his mimicry he becomes eventually a kind of court jester to the court of Salé. His amazing freedom and potential has been converted into art—the only kind of art and the only kind of freedom possible in the feudal system of Salé.

Free in an entirely different way is Ibu, a young girl who had been accused of witchcraft but who escaped from imprisonment in the ju-ju house. Interestingly, her survival after the escape is taken as showing her superiority to the ju-ju and she eventually becomes Elizabeth's apprentice-priestess.

Another accused witch—Osi, the girl rescued by Aladai —shows an opposite development. A spoiled young beauty of her village before the accusation, Osi becomes a prisoner of the ju-ju psychologically as well as physically. Even after her rescue by Aladai and Schlemm she never becomes a fully functioning human being; reduced to irrational terror she has barely enough consciousness to know that she must remain with Aladai. In his company she gains a kind of metaphorical significance, suggesting the lowest level of human exis-

tence. But her urge to survive is closely connected to the
sacrificial urge, and eventually she sacrifices herself to the
river god, under the direction of the blood-obsessed Coker.
Her hold on Aladai obviously comes not only from the pity
that he feels for her. It stems also from his own urge towards
the irrationally sacrificial. It is even possible to argue that
while Ibu is helped to freedom by Musa's creative freedom,
Osi is kept enslaved by Aladai's own slavery. In any case
it is clear that Aladai's relation to the ju-ju is as ambiguous
as his status in Coker's camp, while Osi's imprisonment suggests her submission to it and Ibu's escape suggest her superiority over it.

Whatever the complication of detail, the major confrontation of forces remains that between Aladai and the
British, as shown clearly in the opening scene of invasion.
Among the British there are a number of opposing points of
view, however. The official British representative, Burwash,
the resident, wants to take no action at all, and also wants
no actions to happen without him. As an official in the Service he has a greater stake in preserving the peace than in
achievement, and all his efforts are to avoid a crisis. Unlike
the emir, however, he does not refuse change, as long as it
does not cause a ruckus noticeable by his superiors: "He was,
however, extremely anxious not to have, to use his own
phrase, any unfortunate incidents in his station. He knew
that they would not be liked at headquarters" (18 *Af W*).[7]

The other whites are divided into essentially three
groups: that seen most clearly in Captain Rubin, whose only
connection to events is personal and who is decently concerned with horses, polo, and bagatelle during the revolution;
that seen in Mrs. Pratt and Dick Honeywood, narrow-minded,
and racist, and utterly opposed to any progress by the natives
toward Western civilization; and that seen in Judy Coote,
hoping for the orderly growth of freedom and progress among
the Africans.

Aladai's invasion of the white enclave both at the races
and later at the Scotch Club is, naturally enough, ignored
more or less by Rubin and violently opposed by Honeywood

and Mrs. Pratt, while Judy Coote comes to his rescue and is the only one to relate to him.

The more meaningful opposition among the whites, however, parallels that between the rational Elizabeth and the irrational Coker. This opposition, which runs deeply throughout the book, is the opposition between control and surrender, between logic and terror, between pragmatic reason and irrationality, and it is brought to bear both on Aladai and on his white parallel, Captain Rackham.[8] Among the whites, the irrational is connected with the fundamentalist anarchist, and the Coker-like Mrs. Vowls, "whose crankiness took the common form, among her type, of sentimental anarchism," who believes that "all the evils of the world were due to its Governments" (70 *Af W*), and who tells Aladai that, "We are your worst enemies" (71 *Af W*).

But the prime exemplars of these two views are Judy Coote, an Oxford don, and Dryas Honeywood, who is explicitly associated with Mrs. Vowls by Rackham (268 *Af W*). They stand at either side, not only of the question but also of the two men, Rackham and Aladai. Rackham is caught between the two women. Engaged to the intellectual Judy, he is intensely drawn to the physically agile Dryas. This part of their opposition is seen clearly when they are introduced. Judy is "a little brown woman, with shortsighted brown eyes and a lame leg" (16 *Af W*). Rackham was first attracted by her brains and then came to love her—the order is obviously significant—"for the nature of the judgment, for her capacity to love him, and, at last, for her looks too" (17 *Af W*). Dryas, on the other hand, is his partner in physical games to which he is much drawn. She is first seen delighting in Rackham's race on a dangerous horse, after which she easily beats him at tennis, enchanting him also with her style, "the beauty and strength of her movements" (44 *Af W*). Her physical strength and grace have a more immediate and direct appeal than Judy's intellectual powers, just as Coker's appeal is more immediate than a rational approach.[9]

Dryas first wins the battle for Rackham. That she gets him for her man is secondary in importance to getting him

to lose control in his behavior to Aladai; this is in clear contrast to the way Fisk, another white official, behaves. That
occasion is another invasion of Aladai's. He has been left
alone with Dryas during a trip to Schlemm's mission, partly as
a result of Mrs. Vowls' foolhardiness, and he has landed his
boat, with Dryas aboard, at the private landing of the Hides
company. A great number of Aladai's supporters have gath-
ered to welcome him and a riot is obviously about to occur.
This invasion then is turning into another test of strength,
a confrontation between two powers, even clearer than the
one which began the book and which was averted by Judy's
intercession.

Now Burwash's aide, Fisk, takes it upon himself to avert
the confrontation by intercepting Aladai. He is too late for
that, arriving only as Aladai is already on the wharf, in the
middle of a political speech to his supporters. The conversation between the two men begins as an argument to which
there can be no solution but through violence. " 'Look here,
Mr. Aladai, my orders are to stop your landing.' Aladai
smiled. 'I have landed, you see.' . . . He answered brusquely,
'You *can't* land here, you know. This is a private wharf' "
(203 *Af W*).

It is at this point that a kind of minor miracle happens
and the two opposing forces, the African native prince looking for power, and the British official seeking to prevent him
from getting it, manage to turn to constructive unity through
a leap of imagination. The moment is set off by Aladai's
casual mention of Belton, the public school he had attended
as a youth.

> Aladai's remark instantly made him see the man at
> school: among other boys, white boys like himself. Why,
> there had been a West Indian at his own private school. . . .
> Fisk's sympathies were visual. But they were effective.
> In a moment his whole feeling towards Aladai was changed,
> and, though he did not know it, his voice also changed. He
> said, "Yes, I knew you at Belton. Look here, it seems we're
> in a sort of a fix" (205 *Af W*).

The clue to the change lies in the shift to the first person plural: *we*'re in a fix. The new approach is a practical effort to overcome a difficult situation, one which brings quick results in compromise. Aladai dismisses his mob; in return Aladai is to get an interview with the resident. This logical settlement of the invasion is negated by Rackham's interference at this point. Caught up in an irrational jealousy over Dryas of which he was not quite aware, he physically attacks Aladai, beating him and then knocking him into the river.

Rackham's objection to Aladai, and all such natives who fit into the general category of what he calls "trousered blacks," is never explicitly described, because its nature is essentially irrational. Though at one point he agrees that people like Aladai are really only bad copies of their English counterparts, "Rackham did not really believe that the copies were all bad. His objection was deeper. He did not examine it" (45 *Af W*). His lack of examination is an important element of his feeling, which in the long run is an identification which he cannot accept. If he could examine it, he could either refuse the identification or accept it. Not permitting himself to examine it, he can only react with violent rage. His attitude—similar to that of Kurtz in *Heart of Darkness,* when he says "Exterminate the brutes!" because of his inability to accept his identity with the natives—is seen also when he becomes angry after Judy says that Aladai looked after her. "Judy might have spoken so of himself" (56 *Af W*). Furthermore, what causes him to react so violently is the fact that he is unable to admit fully to himself not only that he is jealous of a black man, but also that he is jealous at all, since he is officially engaged to Judy Coote and the girl in Aladai's boat is Dryas Honeywood.

His blow-up is thus a physical acting out, as irrational as it is self-destructive and deriving from something very close to self-hatred and certainly from an inability to face up to the actual situation.

The same conflict—seen more directly—operates on Aladai and leads to his final and futile invasion, when he and Coker together lead a desperate charge of spearsmen against British soldiers and are both killed.

That he is in the company of Coker is itself a clear indication of his submission to the irrational urge of self-sacrifice. Caught between his intellectual Western education and his emotional Rimi background, one part of him has always been drawn into bloody submission to the ju-ju. His very position as a leader has emphasized the irrational since the crowd wants simply to be led, not to be reasoned with. The ugly beating that Rackham administered in public has helped also to push him away from his Western training. Immediately after the fight he takes off his Western clothing and says, "I am a Rimi man. Take these clothes away and burn them" (210 *Af W*).

More fundamentally, from the beginning Aladai has not been able to distinguish clearly between his responsibility to the Rimi people and to the abstraction of Rimi. From their very first conversation, Judy Coote has emphasized this and has tried to make him see his responsibility to individual persons as a rational, practical one. When Aladai speaks of loving Rimi, she asks, "Rimi—or did you say the Rimi?" and she explains the difference in the most practical terms: "the people have feeling and wants, but I suppose Rimi, strictly speaking, is chiefly silicate mixed with $H_2O$" (106–107 *Af W*). Thus Judy is for the practical benefits that government can give to people: more education, better roads, medicine, and, in general, what Cary thinks of as freedom—the power to make choices.

Dryas, on the other hand, together with Mrs. Vowls, simply believes that all government is inherently evil, without looking at the specific situation, and she tells Aladai so.

Aladai, caught between Judy and Dryas, between Coker and Elizabeth, between reason and irrationality, between politics and the most potent antipolitical view, anarchy, moves in the direction of Dryas and Coker. That is certainly what Cary meant when he said that *The African Witch* "began in a sketch . . . of an African nationalist," describing him also as a "spellbinder" and "hysterical enthusiast." [10]

When he is quite under the spell of Coker he is divided between the two views still but it is the stronger force, emotion, which makes him say, "Rimi, my country—I give my life—for love of Rimi," while it is only his reason which echoes Judy, "That won't do Rimi any good—What Rimi wants is peace, trade—schools—" (293 *Af W*).

At the end, though Aladai has almost forgotten that he wanted to be Emir, he still has to decide whether there is to be a final confrontation or not. Coker, of course, calls for a bloody fight, an invasion by the Rimi which would in effect be suicide. Elizabeth plays practical politics as she has all along, seeking only to achieve her end of making Aladai emir so that her position will be the stronger. Cleverly through her women's war she has turned the tables. Whereas Aladai and Coker only see the strength of their enemy and seek to invade him, that is, to fight violently, she sees the actual physical position and places the women she leads in blocks so that it is the British who seem to do the invading. Since she knows that the British "are too stupid to shoot women" (209 *Af W*), she has made a very strong move. Her acceptance of the ju-ju is just as rational. When Aladai reminds her that one of their aunts jumped into the river to sacrifice herself to the crocodile deity, for the sake of Rimi, she answers pragmatically: "That was for good fishing, and fish came" (211 *Af W*).

The two logical women, Judy and Elizabeth, working together have finally forced Burwash, the man who has until now tried to evade confrontations, by making believe that no issues exist, to agree to a meeting which if held would probably result in giving Aladai the emirate. In contrast to Coker's call for suicidal invasion, they try to introduce a new rational element of cooperation, similar to the one which allowed Fisk to work with Aladai.

Logic, any rational view of the situation, now calls for the meeting, and Judy goes to Aladai to urge it on him. Dryas, however, is there too, and she is there to urge a third course. She calls for an evasion, suggesting that they flee and avoid any meeting. She tells him, "Don't trust anybody—but just escape as soon as you can" (295 *Af W*). When Judy argues, Dryas only says, to support her contention that Aladai cannot trust Burwash, "Look at the Indians and the Irish" (296 *Af W*).

Aladai listens half to her and half to Coker—their voices are similar—and avoids the meeting which would have led to personal achievement for him and a better life for the Rimi, and makes his last, sacrificial invasion, a rush into death, while shouting, ". . . something about Rimi" (298 *Af W*).

These invasions, and the related evasions and imprisonments, are actually workings out of the conflicts which exist in the society of *The African Witch*. There is no reason to insist that as a general pattern for plot this is at all unusual. Traditionally plot is, as Douglas Grant says, "essentially designed to promote conflict; conflict between character and situation, character and character, or within character itself." [11] An examination of Cary's specific emphasis on invasions and the specific conflicts they illustrate, however, helps show the uniquely typical quality of Cary's attitudes and development.

It is worthwhile noting at the beginning that the conflicts are never simply internal, but are always firmly grounded in the sociological and historical situation. Thus Aladai is involved in a political struggle for power, and the details of that struggle involve influences on the characters in such matters as religion, racial feeling, education, and the institutional quality of the African Service, not to mention the individual capacities of individual people.

More specifically, the conflict confronts the old with the new, and the invasion, as a consequence, tends to force the *dynamic* new into a *static* present. Aladai, here, represents a politics which would create change in Rimi, change that is historically progressive. He never articulates a program of government, but he makes it clear that he will emphasize education in order to combat what he sees as the two fundamental evils in Rimi: ignorance and ju-ju (270, and *passim*, *Af W*). [12]

Both the Emir and Salé, in contrast, wish to reduce

change, as well as education. Their control of the feudal power structure is best served by letting things continue as they are. This desire to retain the *status quo* is shared by the British, whose policy at this time is that of indirect rule—a policy which meant in effect as little interference as possible with the rule of the existing Emir.[13] The policy was strengthened, Cary suggests here as elsewhere, by the Western anarchistic impulse which holds as evil not only all government, but all of Western civilization as well. The anarchist mind therefore wants to see the native African remain in his pre-Westernized condition or, in the terms of *The African Witch,* without trousers. This is the initial attitude of Marie Hasluck, the anarchist of *An American Visitor.*

A major effort at Westernizing the Africans will naturally cause dynamic and far-reaching changes with general social effect, and corresponding personal effect as well. An example in *The African Witch* is that of Musa, the young boy whose creative imagination finds no constructive outlet in the static Rimi, and who winds up as the court jester. Another example is Akande Tom, whose desire for Westernization almost leads to the destruction of the ju-ju house.

It is no accident that the Africans who support Westernization—for instance Mr. Johnson, or the Christians of *Aissa Saved*—tend to be like Musa, those who are on the fringes of their own native culture, unable to find room for development within it.

An even clearer case of the dynamically new invading the static is that of the road in *Mister Johnson.* The road, a structural center of that book in several ways, is opposed by the conservative emir, and brought to fruition by the dynamic Johnson. When it finally is built it seems to say to Rudbeck, the British district officer, "I'm smashing up the old Fada— I shall change everything and everybody in it. I am abolishing the old ways, the old ideas, the old law; I am bringing wealth and opportunity for good as well as vice, new powers to men and therefore new conflicts. I am the revolution" (168–69 *Mr J*).

In each case, the invader is also the more dynamic per-

sonality. Thus Aladai is personally more dynamic than Burwash or the emir or Salé; Johnson is more dynamic than any
character in his book; the native Christians in *Aissa Saved*
are more dynamic than the followers of the local goddess
Oke. The exception is Monkey Bewsher in *An American
Visitor,* who is personally the most dynamic character, but
yet opposes the invasion of the tin miners who are led by
the far less dynamic Cottee. But the case there is more complicated than it seems at first; Bewsher is opposing the invasion of Western business and religion, it is true, but at the
same time he himself is an invader of his pagan Birri trying
—with ironic success, it turns out—to manufacture for them
a new nationalism and a new religion.

Bewsher is an exceptional case, in that he is a dynamic
figure whose historical view is regressive. Ordinarily the dynamic has the forward thrust of history in the sense that it
pushes Westernization into the African social structure—
Christianity in the case of *Aissa Saved,* business in the case of
*An American Visitor,* imperialism with its complexities in
*Castle Corner,* all of them connected with Western education,
Western science, the Western emphasis on *things,* and the
greater potential for change and conflict in Western culture.
The books show such invasion to be both desirable and unavoidable. They assume that whatever shortcomings British
culture has, its introduction into Africa brings an increase of
cultural and personal freedom. As Aladai says in supporting
his call for Western education, "what should I be if it [Rimi
education] was all I had—rubbing my nose in the dirt in front
of Elizabeth's ju-ju? Don't be sentimental about our Rimi
education. . . ." (68 *Af W*). Rubbing his nose in front of
Elizabeth's ju-ju is exactly what Akande Tom does because
he does not have enough education. The cruelty, the murder,
the missed opportunities, the closing off of life to potentially
talented individuals everywhere in the Africa that is still unchanged shows Westernization to be a progressive step. British
policy may be a muddle, British officials may be foolish, British teachings may lead to entirely unexpected results, but
nevertheless, in all the African books, the general effect of

British imperialism leads to an increase of freedom, an expansion of possibility, that is, and of greater choice for the individuals involved.

Historically, the confrontations are, in the long run, as unavoidable as the future itself. Cottee, in *An American Visitor,* says in criticism of Bewsher's attempts to evade confrontation, "even if civilization meant for the Birri a meaner, shallower kind of life, how could any man hope to fight against it when *it came with the whole drive of the world behind it. . . .*" (234 *Am V,* my italics). In *Castle Corner* Felix's dream of a world without conflict is spoken of half comically as "a universal Oxford . . . where the worst conflict would be a college football match . . ." (86–87 *CC*).

The attempt to avoid confrontation is actually an attempt to avoid reality. Bewsher's attempt to keep the Birri out of the "general flux," [14] Mrs. Pratt's hope to keep the natives out of the European sector, Burwash's attempts to avoid issues, and Dryas' successful try to keep Aladai from his meeting—these are all denials of dynamic forces which really do exist. Confrontation is necessary, but not especially because sometimes men can leap beyond their circumstances and take up common cause, as in the case of Fisk's confrontation with Aladai. Such cooperation is by far the exception. Confrontation is necessary for a much more basic reason: reality is built out of opposition and it demands the possibility of conflict, the critical moment when the actual forces confront each other.

As a matter of fact, the confrontations test the reality and strength of the forces, and thus they also have a pedagogic quality. For instance, in Aladai's final suicidal attempt to invade the British system, reality rushes in, as it were, with the bullet that kills him. A meeting with Burwash would have confronted his opposition with his strength, his rational control against the weakness of the ju-ju. Instead he chooses an action which has no bearing on the real facts. The confrontation is not one which can lead to progressive movement. It simply opposes Aladai's weakness—his irrational instinct—with a stronger, but nonrational force, the unthinking police.

The incident stands in direct and formal contrast to Aladai's success in his invasion of the town when he fought the supporters of Salé. Then, though totally surrounded by enemies, he was unharmed and a spear hit him without doing any damage. At that time, however, he was opposing the ju-ju, opposing the conservative forces of Salé, in short he was using his rational strength (49–56 *Af W*).

The lesson is a little drastic for Aladai, since it kills him in the process of teaching. Exactly similar in this sense is the death of Monkey Bewsher at the hand of one of his most promising pupils, Obai. Bewsher has been trying to teach his pagans to become nationalists, and to isolate them so that they will be free from either submission to the British, or from conflict with them. He tried, in other words, to do the impossible, to avoid the forces which really are the operating ones. His pupil, Obai, finally does learn the lesson of nationalism, not for the sake of progress but for the sake of opposition to Bewsher himself. Just before he kills Bewsher, he screams Bewsher's nationalist catch phrase, "Birri for the Birri," but he couples it with another, "Kill the whites" (228 *Am V*).

Bewsher's death also teaches a lesson to his wife, Marie Hasluck. Her mistake here was that she held a false view of faith, love, and trust in God. That is why she refuses to give Bewsher the pistol which might have saved his life. Of course, Marie is not altogether wrong; love and trust in God are real forces, but they are not of the sort that are able to stand up against physical facts such as spears.

The missionary Schlemm is involved in a similar lesson. When one of his native students hits him on the nose, Schlemm receives with the blow a "shock to his ideals" (218 *Af W*). In general, Schlemm knows a great deal more than the other whites. He is the only one, for instance, to have an inkling of the ju-ju trials held by Elizabeth and of the true tensions among the natives. Nevertheless, he is "an idealist" —that is, he could not quite believe that one of his own pupils would participate in violence. Schlemm refuses to learn the lesson, preferring to pretend that the blow was an accident.

The other missionaries in *The African Witch*, the Fortts, suffer the consequences of ignorance. They never knew that Coker preached his own kind of Christianity to their converts, in an abandoned ju-ju house a scant mile from their mission. When their congregation disappears to hear Coker demand their destruction, they don't even know enough to be alarmed. They are killed, and when Schlemm returns, he is killed too.

The situation is almost exactly the same as the one in *Aissa Saved*, where the missionaries, the Carrs, are also unaware of the native gathering place parallel to theirs, the place where the riots which are the basis of the book are planned (127 *AS*). In each of these cases at the moment of confrontation, reality invades ignorance or mistaken beliefs in order to show the actual nature of the forces operating.

## II

As such confrontations stress the violence of the opposed forces of society, the general view given by Cary's early books is one of revolution and murder, in which people are ready to shoot real bullets at real people for their religion or for their political views. Though the religious, political, and social views—not to mention the insight into character—are far from simple in these books, they are nevertheless very directly and very simply opposed, and thus the conflict between them is emphasized. In later works the conflicts remain, indeed they are largely the same ones; but they are shown not so much in opposition as in *juxtaposition* to each other.

The early African novels emphasize the moment of crisis, of potential change, and their typical form is an invading one. The later works emphasize the total situation at any given moment, a situation which includes within itself a variety of forces.

Partly, no doubt, the shift in emphasis follows naturally the shift in scene from Africa to Europe. In Africa conflicts are more likely to be resolved by violence, especially in Cary's

Africa where the social and political structure is in the process of fundamental change.[15] In addition there is a shift in
technique from the more direct, the more obvious, to the less
direct and the less obvious. Finally, there is also a shift in
fundamental emphasis in the works, a shift from division to
unity. But the unity is one uniquely peculiar to Cary and
paradoxically it insists on its own multiplicity.

The trilogies—representing Cary's major work after the
thirties—show the change most clearly.[16] Both trilogies are
unusual in that they are neither strictly circular nor strictly
sequential. That is, they do not cover what is essentially the
same ground, usually with psychological emphasis, from three
separate points of view (as does *Rashomon,* perhaps the best
known example of the type), nor do they simply follow each
other in time, usually with sociological and historical emphasis, as *Men of Good Will* does.[17] Instead, they present a situation which is only very loosely similar in the separate books,
told from the conflicting viewpoints of three separate narrators. The purpose in each case is not so much to throw light
on the actual events—not even to question them—as much as
it is to throw light on the nature of the view which each
character has, and how it affects the others. Each individual
volume is essentially an *apologia*—a conscious attempt by each
character to explain his general attitude toward life. The
trilogies as a whole, however, gain their effect from the juxtaposition of the separate works. Each character's view is different, sometimes radically different, but each view combines
with the others—unwilling though the combination may be—
to produce the total situation.[18]

Thus, the first trilogy carefully presents three characters,
each talking in his own voice and each describing his own
world. In a sense they are each one aspect of man, with the
usual double implication of that phrase: there is a bit of
each in every man, while every man tends to be primarily one
of the three.

Thus, Wilcher, the narrator of *To Be a Pilgrim,* is the
conserver of the past; Gulley Jimson, the artist narrator of
*The Horse's Mouth,* is the destroyer of the past and creator of

the future; while Sara Monday, the narrator of *Herself Surprised,* is the nester woman who makes herself and her family comfortable wherever she is.

By another, related set of categories Wilcher is the Blakean Urizen, Gulley is Los, and Sara is a female will.[19]

It is Sara, as mistress to both, who brings together the two men who would otherwise never have known each other. She joins them, too, in the other more allegorical sense, since she represents the natural need of man for family and for the inspiriting quality that the woman gives to man.

Her language and her imagery are drawn from the kitchen and from the flesh, reflecting an eye that carefully observes the physical reality around her. Her vocabulary, like her thoughts, is full of money, of food, of furnishings and possessions. But most of all, it is the language and consciousness of flesh and the body which is typical of her; hence she even discusses the artistic creativity of Gulley Jimson in terms of the regularity of his stool (117 *HS*). Her first description of herself comes at the very beginning of the book, when she first surprises herself in a mirror on her honeymoon in Paris. "Look at that fat, common trollop of a girl with a snub nose and the shiny cheeks jumping out of her skin to be in a Paris hat" (10 *HS*). Along with the emphasis on the physical, the self-denigrating tone is typical, too, and is developed throughout the work in the tradition of the didactic literature of the fallen sinner who uses her own sinful career as a warning to her reader.[20] Her interest in her body makes her apply the admonition of the prison chaplain, "Know thyself," to the flesh:

> "Know thyself," the chaplain says, and it is true that I never knew myself till now. Yet I thought I knew myself very well, and that I was humble enough, and I remember the first time I saw myself in my own true body (9–10 *HS*).

This passage at the very opening of the book, is parallel to the closing paragraph which mixes her concern with money, her flesh, her relation to society, and her morality:

A good cook will always find work, even without a character, and can get a new character in twelve months, and better herself, which, God helping me, I shall do, and keep a more watchful eye, next time, on my flesh, now I know it better (220 *HS*).

Love for her flesh also causes her death, since Gulley kills her—half accidentally—when she refuses to give him the paintings, which she loves mostly for their fleshiness.

This murder, it should be emphasized, does not at all have the same effect as the violence in the earlier books. It does not imply the victory of one force over another, as when the British soldiers kill Aladai, for instance. Rather it suggests the eternal relationship between the two principles of woman nest maker and creator-destroyer. It is in the nature of the artist to destroy the forms of the past, and it is in nature of the free man to destroy the woman who has captured him.

On the contrary, the murder itself indicates the curiously lasting quality of their relationship. Their relationship on the personal level (as Gulley and Sara), on the allegorical level (as nest maker and creator-destroyer), and on the social level (as classless artist and lower-middle-class servant with the responsibility to make money and be respectable) is a continuing one even after the murder. The two need each other, and Gulley's vision of Sara after her death strongly suggests this. Perhaps if the universe were otherwise organized and there were no such need, things would be better. They are not otherwise organized however. And that, as a matter of fact, is probably the largest point of *The Horse's Mouth,* the book which insists, more clearly than others of Cary's, on the need to accept things as they are.

Personally, socially, and allegorically, Gulley is contrasted to Wilcher, the upper-class conserver of society, as well as made complementary to him. Neither likes the other, and Gulley's description of Wilcher makes the point: "Genus, Boorjwar; species Blackcoatius Begoggledus Ferocissimouse. All eaten up with lawfulness and rage" (183 *HM*). On the other hand their conflict, too, is not a final one. The formal result is that when Gulley enters Wilcher's house, there is no quality of invasion to the act, in the sense of the African books; there is no full confrontation of opposing forces. Rather the two men who do not like each other make a deal, almost a legitimate business deal, so that Gulley gets a monthly retainer in order to leave Sara alone.

Wilcher's typical language shows his attempt to gather spiritual meaning out of possessions, not the small possessions of Sara which give comfort to the flesh, but the large possessions—his family estate, Tolbrook, for instance—which are associated with the upper class and which represent power. His language is generally abstract and completely skips over that bodily level which is so much a part of Sara. Indeed, he hardly mentions at all the sexual indiscretions which nearly land him in jail a number of times, though he seems to feel perfectly free to suggest his burning down of houses. Similarly, in bed with either of his mistresses, Sara and Julie, he is never seen as discussing anything other than his main preoccupations: property and the spirit.

He is hardly ever seen as acting—except in an underhanded way which surprises even him when he becomes fully aware of it. Rather, he is acted upon, and watches the actions of his more involved brothers and sister, the aesthetic, intellectual Edward, the soldier, man-of-action Bill, and the anarchic-religious Lucy. When he does act it is often as parody (for instance when he dresses up as an Indian and missionary); at other times it is disastrous (for instance when he addresses the wrong crowd for Edward's campaign). His affair with Julie is also in the nature of a parody of Edward's success. He even plays a parody of family life, and he is very much concerned with children, none of whom, of course, are his. Indeed there is a kind of terrible irony in this allegorical description of the British, upper-class gentleman, the preserver of the society who has no organic relation to what he is conserving but is rather the weighted-down victim of his possessions and his own lack of vitality.

The double time sequence of Wilcher's book—in his narration he lives as much in the past as in the present—

parallels his division between the material and the spiritual. The first impression is that he sees a spiritual essence in the past, while the present is a sad loss. His point of view gradually changes, however, with his participation in the affair of Robert and Ann. At the very end of the book he accepts the spiritual essence as existing in the present and he looks toward the future. He has just told his niece, Ann, that she takes life too seriously, and she asks:

> "Don't you think it's rather serious?"
> "My dear child, you're not thirty yet. You have forty, forty-five years in front of you."
> "Yes" (342 *TB P*).

The quality of her final "yes" is ambiguous, and there is no certainty whether she is agreeing therapeutically with a sick man, or agreeing to life. His positive acceptance of life at this point is, however, unambiguously clear.[21]

Gulley Jimson, of the three, is most conscious of language; he manipulates it as an artist does, making metaphor out of everything he sees (and his visual capacity is extraordinary); he shapes myth out of idea, and poetry out of sound.

Gulley—the creator who is also destroyer—is the most energetic of the three characters, and his language reflects this, as can be seen in the incomplete sentences of the book's opening:

> I was walking by the Thames. Half-past morning on an autumn day. Sun in a mist. Like an orange in a fried fish shop. All bright below. Low tide, dusty water and a crooked bar of straw, chicken-boxes, dirt and oil from mud to mud. Like a viper swimming in skim milk. The old serpent, symbol of nature and love (11 *HM*).

His language is, in addition, filled with violence as well as with rage, often coupled with the attempt to suppress them. When he is discussing his destroyed picture, the Fall, for instance, he makes a characteristic criticism—his painting, he says, wasn't solid enough. ". . . what was the Fall after all. The discovery of the solid hard world, good and evil. Hard as rocks and sharp as poisoned thorns" (173 *HM*). A few sentences later he describes the process of falling in love:

> Boys and girls fall in love, that is, they are driven mad and go blind and deaf and see each other not as human animals with comic noses and bandy legs and voices like frogs, but as angels so full of shining goodness that like hollow turnips with candles put in them, they seem miracles of beauty. And the next minute the candles shoot out sparks and burn their eyes. And they seem to each other like devils, full of spite and cruelty (173 *HM*).

Repeatedly, his visual imagery focuses on burning things; for instance, spring trees are "burning in the evening sun" (193 *HM*). It is the same pattern in his personality which makes him see whatever is desirable in art as solid, heavy, hard, as when Gulley is for once seriously discussing art.[22] The question there is whether the work of a young sculptor is "chunky" enough, whether it has "the weight" (202 *HM*). Bad art on the other hand is the opposite, and Gulley says of Lady Beeder's work that "when people try to hang their hats and umbrellas on a Beeder, they may find a sort of an absence" (148 *HM*). Scenes he finds not useful for his art he describes as "sausage," implying softness as well as a machine-made mixture (62 *HM*).

Part of his pattern of violence is the result of his unsuccessful relationship to society.[23] Knowing himself to be devoted to art, and seriously concerned for his work, he is yet ignored by the social system and forced to spend much of his time just getting the basic necessities of food, shelter, and the tools of his trade: paints, brushes, canvas. At the same time the society has no interest or understanding of what he is trying to achieve. His rage at times like these is understandable—even quite apart from his specifically violent personality. Yet he also knows that he has a job to do, painting, and that if he lets himself go he will spend his time fighting rather than working. Sara, in her book, has already described his refusal to take what seemed to her logical and practical steps to become successful. Here he is continually caught between the impulse to rage and the impulse to keep quiet and do his work. The theme comes to its strongest expression just after Gulley is running away from London, after the Beeders come home to the apartment which he has thoroughly ransacked and emptied in order to give these millionaire inhabitants of the land of Beulah a painting of the raising of Lazarus which they do not at all want. He expresses both his potential rage and his need to contain it:

> "If I wasn't a reasonable man," I said to Nosy, "I should get annoyed with Governments and the People and the World, and so on. I should get into a state and wish that the silly bitch had a nose so that I could kick it between the eyes. I should say that bugs have better manners and lice have more distinguished minds" (219 *HM*).

But just as he is growing excited he gets what seems to him like a stroke, and he regains control of himself:

> "Hold me up, Nosy, and keep cool. No malice intended. Revenge has a green face, he feeds on corpses. . . . They nearly knocked me off my pins," I said. "Put me into a temper. But by God, I beat 'em . . . I forgive 'em, Nosy. And tomorrow I shall forget 'em" (219–20 *HM*).

Such suppression of rage, for the sake of surviving and doing the job, is a theme that runs throughout the entire book. It is one of the bases of the argument between Plant and Gulley. Plant's Spinozist view that the world is just and has meaning —though beyond men's understanding—would certainly lead Gulley to grievances he cannot afford. Gulley prefers Blake's rejection of such terms for an insistence on personal freedom, which allows Gulley to create in spite of the injustice. It is also the basis of a good portion of his relationship with Coker, who is a kind of female Plant in this context, wishing to suffer out of pride, believing in God, and ultimately, in justice as well. It was also one of his running arguments with Sara, and it was that which led to "Boko on the toko," the worst beating of all those he gave her, after which he also left her. She wants to fight when the wall painting on which she has staked a great deal and which he has been working on for

years is destroyed—"Painting is my job, not fighting," Gulley
says then. "The only thing for us, Sall, is to keep serene and
spit on the lot of them" (132 *HS*). It is a measure of the great
difficulty he has keeping this balance that he does hit her
when she keeps after him.

Besides this rage, his language contains the energy of
poetry. He uses analogy constantly, for instance when he describes Hickson's eyes as "a pair of half sucked acid drops,"
(101 *HM*) or when he describes the people who come to
Plant's lecture in terms of fish:

> The people kept floating in. Like fish in an aquarium
> full of dirty brown water, three dimensions of fish faces,
> every one on top of other. Bobbing slowly to and fro, and
> up and down. Goggle eyes, cod mouths. Hanging in the
> middle of the brown. Waiting for a worm or just suspended.
> Old octopus in corner with a green dome and a blue beak,
> working his arms. Trying to take off his overcoat without
> losing his chair. Old female in black with a red nose creeping
> about in the dark corners like a crawfish, shaking her bonnet
> feathers and prodding her old brown umbrella at the chairs
> (74 *HM*).

He is carefully aware of rhythm, as well as of puns—
as in his description of the Beeder art collection:

Usual modern collection. Wilson Steer, water in water-
colour, Matthew Smith, victim of the crime in slaughter-
colour; Utrillo whitewashed wall in mortarcolour; Matisse,
odalisque in scortacolour; Picasso, spatchcock horse in torta-
colour; Gilbert Spencer, cocks and prigs in thoughtacolour;
Stanley Spencer, cottage garden in hortacolour; Braque, half
a bottle of half and half in portercolour; William Roberts,
pipe dream in snortercolour; Wadsworth, rockses, blockses
and fishy boxes all done by self in nautacolour; Duncan
Grant, landscape in strawtacolour; Frances Hodgkin, cows
and wows and frows and sows in chortacolour; Roualt, per-
ishing Saint in fortacolour; Epstein, Leah waiting for Jacob
in squawtacolour. All the most high-toned and expensive
(146 *HM*).[24]

These devices are more like tricks, personal traits of speech. A more fundamental pattern of Gulley's way of talking and thinking is his habit of correcting exaggerations, of reversing hyperbole. When he has first come out of prison, for instance, and finds his painting of the Fall damaged, and all his supplies stolen, he notices the irony inherent in the conflict between himself and the way of life reality has been forcing on him. "Here am I, I said, Gulley Jimson, whose pictures have been bought by the nation, or sold at Christie's by millionaires for hundreds of pounds, pictures which were practically stolen from me, and I haven't a brush or a tube of colour." He catches himself, however, a few sentences later, partly in his usual way of not permitting himself to get up a grievance, but also partly for the sake of the truth. "I mustn't exaggerate. The nation has got only one of my pictures which was left it by will and which quite likely it didn't want; and only one millionaire has ever bought my stuff. Also he took a big risk of losing his money. Also he is probably far from being a millionaire" (15 *HM*). Similarly when he is in prison again—having for once given way to his rage and thrown a snuff box through Hickson's window—and gets a letter suggesting a critical biographical study of his works, he is tempted in his usual ironic fashion to think of himself as an important artist. "Old horse, you are now famous. The dealers will be running after you with cheques in one hand and smiles in the other. You will have commissions to pick. And the walls will come waltzing to your big front door. As many as you like." But, then he calls attention to where he is and what he is doing in prison as a painter. "As I was an artist, I had been, put on to painter's work, whitewashing. Latrines, etc." (112 *HM*). Similarly when in one of the book's most serious passages, Gulley is walking with Nosy and is outlining his ideas about the painting he has finished and the one he is about to start, and is incidentally explaining his basic beliefs about the nature of freedom, his freewheeling ideas are continually offset by the amazed stuttering of Nosy on the one hand, and on the other, by the actual physical circumstances

they are both in. Ironically, while Gulley is describing his
beliefs about the nature of freedom, he is walking about in
a storm because he has no money at all and no place to go:

> "The fallen man—nobody's going to look after him. The
> poor bastard is free—a free and responsible citizen. The Fall
> into freedom. Yes, I might call it the Fall into Freedom."
>
> "F—f—free," said Nosy, with his eyes starting out of his
> head. For he didn't know what I was talking about.
>
> "Yes," I said. "Free to cut his bloody throat, if he likes,
> or understand the bloody world, if he likes, and cook his
> breakfast with hell-fire, if he likes, and construct for himself
> a little heaven of his own, if he likes, all complete with a
> pig-faced angel and every spiritual pleasure including the
> joys of love; or also, of course, he can build himself a little
> hell full of pig-faced devils and all material miseries includ-
> ing the joys of love. . . ."

While Gulley is continuing in this vein, Nosy again interrupts: " 'The f-f-fall into f-f-f,' said Nosy. . . ." And this
ironic comment is followed by a description of the scene: "I
threw the water out of my hat and once more it fell down the
opening of my waistcoat" (173–74 *HM*).

Such continually repeated deflations of Gulley in his relations to society and to his art are matched by the deflations
of his own hyperbole. When he is in the middle of his last
wallpainting, the Creation, he stops off at the Feathers, where
a cat becomes a metaphor for existential being. She is, "the
only individual cat in the world. Universal cat" (286 *HM*),
she is associated with Blake's Tiger, as well as with Sara Monday and she is seen, like all of physical reality in this book,
as one of the paths towards spiritual essence. The next to last
image of the section therefore shows the cat apocalyptically.
But then the metaphor is tied back again to the literal:

> As I slipped out, something like a fiery comet whizzed
> past my left ear and I saw old Snow land in the light in front
> of me; all four feet at once. And then with one spring, in
> every joyful lovely muscle, ascend into Heaven; or the garden
> wall (288 *HM*).

The last phrase is the typical Gulley deflation, which can also be seen in the moment when Gulley reaches both his highest and lowest state as he is in the middle of his final and greatest work, the Creation. This painting, which gains metaphorical and psychological meaning for Gulley because it is a pure creation, is destroyed while it is created, as the wall on which it is built is torn down by the town council while Gulley is painting.[25] For the anarchist destructive-creator there can be no higher creation. It is especially meaningful to Gulley that in the act of destruction the center of the composition, a whale, seems to come alive:

> And just then the whale smiled. Her eyes grew bigger and brighter and she bent slowly forward as if she wanted to kiss me. I had a shock.

Gulley is not quite ready at this time to deflate himself. Indeed, he is trying to make the entire pattern of defeat into a triumph of acceptance and thus a triumph of the creative spirit. Even when he sees the wall collapse and notices a crowd standing around laughing, he sees them first as angels laughing at what "must be a work of eternity, a chestnut, a horse-laugh." And even when he realizes they are laughing at him, he is ready to work this into his framework of accept-ance. "I should have got up and bowed if my swing had been steady enough" (295 *HM*). It is at this time that Gulley is deflated, by mortality itself, as he suffers a stroke.

Parallel to this pattern of exaggeration corrected by real-ity, there is a pattern of pretence in Gulley's character and language, a pattern which is related to the question of his identity, his worth as an artist and his place as a human being. In one of the first scenes in the book, Gulley telephones Hickson in the voice of the president of the Royal Academy (17 *HM*). He repeats this kind of pretence a number of times, speaking as a more important member of the society than he really is, partly for the joke, but partly also because he somehow feels that he might possibly get something out of it. Thus when he does talk to Hickson as the president he is having fun, and he is hounding a man whom in one sense he considers an enemy who has gotten his paintings without paying enough for them, but also he thinks there just might be some money in it. There is something of the same ambiguity in his pose as the Artful Dodger. When he is arrested he tells the police, "Be careful what you're doing. I'm Mister Gulley Jimson, and I shall put this matter into my lawyer's hands. First-class lawyers. For false imprisonment and assault. Obviously you don't know who I am. Call a taxi" (110 *HM*). The irony of the statement here is that they do not, in fact, know who Gulley is, nor does anyone else. And Gulley does not always quite know either. He does not ever quite know what his own standing as an artist is. He frequently adopts the pose of a successful bourgeois painter, partly in the hopes that this will sell more paintings. When he first meets the critic Alabaster, for instance, he pretends to be in great demand for this reason: "I have just completed the finest thing I ever did. It only wants a touch. An important work. Nine by twelve. Of course a lot of people are after it, and the Chantry trustees would jump at it for the nation" (145 *HM*). In the same speech he willingly denies that the picture is the Fall, even though he believes that it is the greatest thing he's done. He does exactly the same thing when he is in the middle of his final work, the Creation, and he is visited by a delegation which wants him to do a portrait. He tells them what the picture means "with my best social manner, which I believe is not unworthy of a President of the Salon or the memory of Charles Peace in the dock" (274 *HM*). He can also speak like an art critic (he calls them "crickets") when he is not seriously engaged. When he is copying his own early painting of Sara in the bath—in a style he has long since grown beyond—he describes it ironically as

> bearing on its face all those indubitable marks which as the crickets say, testify to that early freshness of vision and bravura of execution which can never be imitated by a hand which in acquiring a mature decision of purpose, has lost, nevertheless, that *je ne sais quoi*, without which perhaps no work of art is entitled to the name of genius (264 *HM*).

When he gets more involved, however, he cannot quite carry off the pretence. When, for instance, he criticises the watercolors of Lady Beeder, he knows very well that it will pay him to talk nicely of the pictures. He has even discussed with Alabaster a deal to put out a fake "Life and Works of Lady Flora Beeder" for the cash in it (147 *HM*). But partly because of his real concern with art, and probably even more because of his programmatic self-destructive urge, he cannot go completely through with the pretence. He stops his polite-nesses to tell her what he really feels: the sky of which she is so proud he calls "a bit accidental, like when the cat spills its breakfast" (152 *HM*). He goes on to tell her what she has absolutely no interest in hearing, that real art is not pretty and beyond technique:

> All this amateur stuff is like farting Annie Laurie through a keyhole. It may be clever but is it worth the trouble? What I say is, why not do some real work, your ladyship? Use your loaf, I mean your brain. Do some thinking. Sit down and ask yourself what's it all about (153 *HM*).

His concern for his own views of art—pushing him be-yond the practically advantageous, just as his aesthetics are themselves resolutely impractical in the sense that they push him into the new, the untried and the self-destructive—is also a concern for his position as an artist, and his many poses as a successful bourgeois artist are never completely false. He really does wonder about his position as an artist, as his only half ironic question to the Beeders shows:

> "What you think I been doing all my life—playing tiddly winks with little Willie's first colour-box? Why friends," I appealed to their better halves, "what do you see before you, a lunatic with lice in his shirt and bats in his clock (this was for her ladyship on the maternal side) a poodle faking crook that's spent fifty years getting nothing for nothing and a kick up below for interest on the investment (this was for Sir William on the side of business commonsense), or somebody that knows some thing about his job? (153 *HM*).

Of course the point is that Gulley is never quite sure which one of these he is. And his quick shifts between the one view of himself and the other, his ability to adopt first one of these poses and then the other suggests the uncertainty. As for the reader, he winds up fairly well convinced that Gulley is both.

Parallel to his role as artist—whether the pose is that of the great genius, the craftsman who cares nothing for success, or the bourgeois artist who thinks only of commissions and his place in the academy—Gulley also adopts the role of the anti-art Philistine who has so embittered his own life. His relation to Nosy, for instance, is continually that of a Dutch uncle warning off a young relative from an unsafe course in art to a safe practical life in the Civil Service (158–64 HM). Similarly, he insists on describing his own career as an artist as a misfortune that happened to him and that he was unable to avoid (60–65 HM). To Plant, who tries to take a high-minded, moral view of art—"what is an artist for, but to make us see the beauty of the world?" (70 HM)—Gulley says: "What is art? Just self-indulgence. You give way to it. It's a vice. Prison is too good for artists—they ought to be rolled down Primrose Hill in a barrel full of broken bottles once a week and twice on public holidays, to teach them where they get off" (70 HM).

The rhetorical exaggerations offset by reality and the pretences—in which different elements of the man offset each other—are all of a piece in Gulley, and they both relate directly to his symbolic vision of art. His art as such is always moving between the vision of the eye and the vision of the soul, between realism and symbolism, between the individual and the typical. Each woman he sees is to him part of the archetype, and as such each is also part of his picture of Eve. When he sees Lady Beeder, for instance, he sees her as "more beautiful than true" (155 HM).[26]

What eyes. Grey like a night full of moonlight and pencilled all about with radiating strokes of blue-grey like the shading of petals. Darkening to the outer edges of the iris as if the colour had run there and set. A white as bright as a cloud; lashes, two pen strokes of the new bronze, dark as sunrise before a single ray reaches the ground. And what a nose, what lips. Eve. Fearful symmetry (155 *HM*).

Both Sara—who serves Gulley as model and archetype—and Coker suggest parts of Eve to Gulley, and at one point he speaks of using Coker's arm with Sara's body (92 *HM*).

Gulley transmutes not only from the material into the spiritual but back the other way too, as when he translates Blake's lyrics into pragmatic terms. First he quotes Blake:

> For every generated body in its inward form
> Is a garden of delight and a building of magnificence
> Built by the sons of Los
> And the herbs and flowers and furniture and beds and
>     chambers
> Continually woven in the looms of Enitharmon's
>     daughters.
> In bright cathedron's golden domes with care and love
>     and tears.

He continues with his translation:

> That is to say, old Billy Blake dreamed dreams while Mrs.
> Blake emptied the pot (41 *HM*).

His paintings are essentially attempts to create several simultaneous levels of experience: to portray the individual quality of the object painted (mimesis), to create a formal unity (form), and to give it mythical meaning (archetype). Thus when he looks at his painting of the Fall he admires the leg he has done: "it's leggy all right. If that limb could speak, it would say, 'I walk for you, I run for you, I kneel for you. But I have my self-respect' " (15 *HM*). That is to say, the leg has the archetypal quality of legginess, while it has the mimetic quality of an individual leg at the same time. But he is simultaneously concerned with form as well, and quite aside from any mimetic or archetypal requirements, he thinks that "The serpent wants to be a bit thicker, and I could bring his tail round to make a nice curl over the tree"

(15 *HM*). Such formal concerns are frequently repeated in his musings over his work. About the same picture he says, for instance, "the serpent will have to come a little behind Adam to avoid two cylinders meeting at the vertical. All right, make the serpent fatter—fatter than Adam. Fat and stiff—erect. And all those red scales against Adam's blue-white flesh" (29 *HM*).[27]

As an artist, Gulley is able even to transmute human suffering into the formal frame of his art, as when a bar conversation of a deaf girl leads him to a formal visual construction:

> And I saw all the deaf, blind, ugly, cross-eyed, limp-legged, bulge-headed, bald and crooked girls in the world, sitting on little white mountains and weeping tears like sleet. There was a great clock ticking and every time it ticked the tears all fell together with a noise like broken glass tinkling in a plate (21–22 *HM*).

Gulley is classical in insisting—with Sidney—that art captures the true ideal form of objects which are otherwise seen only in their individual accidental appearance. Thus when Coker, seeing his picture of Sara, describes it as "a fat totty in her kinsay" (99 *HM*), Gulley explains that, "you feel the bath, the chair, the towel, the carpet, the bed, the jug, the window, the fields and the woman as themselves. But not as any old jug and woman. But the jug of jugs and the woman of woman" (100 *HM*).

In taking the further step of insisting that art opens the way into the human constant—the archetype—as well, Gulley quotes Blake again:

> And every space smaller than a globule of man's
>    blood opens
> Into eternity of which this vegetable earth is but
>    a shadow.

This means, Gulley says, that

> a jug can be a door if you open it. And a work of imagination opens it for you. And then you feel with all the women that

ever lived and all the women that are ever going to live, and you feel their feeling while they are alone with themselves—in some chosen private place, bathing, drying, dressing, criticizing, touching, admiring themselves safe behind locked doors. Nothing there but women's feeling and woman's beauty and critical eye (100 *HM*).

His view is thus the consciously articulated one of the symbolists, and he speaks of Blake as a symbolist: "What is Nature to a man like old Billy Blake. To the imagination of genius. A door to glory" (224 *HM*). For Gulley, too, reality has this connection to glory, a connection made visible through the product of the imagination, art. At the same time—and in this too he is like Blake—he insists on the physical reality of the universe and of the individual human experience. He may be a symbolist, but he is far from being a mystic who would deny the ordinary reality. If he sees the typical human quality, the eternity, the glory, behind the jug, then it still continues to remain a jug nevertheless. And the cat may well be ascending into heaven; but it is nonetheless jumping up the garden wall.

This hard headed jumping between the ideal and the real—Blakean and Thoreauvian, too—is the basis of the double pattern of Gulley's language and vision. It explains his exaggeration and his puncturing of it, his dreaming and his waking life, his clear vision and his visionary quality. Through it all, Gulley is looking for the essential reality of the universe, and the closest he can get to it is in his paintings which combine the two levels—though never satisfactorily—and also in his frequently repeated tautologies, the point of which is to insist on essence. Life, he says, is "Practically a MATTER OF LIFE AND DEATH" (292 *HM*), "BE FRIENDS WITH YOUR FRIENDS" (279 *HM*), "IT'S WISE TO BE WISE" (123 *HM*). Blake's view of human freedom—as opposed to Spinoza's view of man's impersonal and unknowable relationship to justice which is looking "ON THE OUTSIDE" (103 *HM*)—is a view from the inside, where you see "the works—it's SOMETHING THAT GOES ON GOING ON" (104 *HM*).

Gulley Jimson is certainly the most dynamic and the most complete character in the first trilogy, perhaps in the entire Cary work. As a result he has been emphasized in studies and in discussions of Cary. Nevertheless he is only one of three major characters and takes his place as one part of the triptychlike trilogy. Perhaps, like the leg in the Fall, Gulley sticks out a bit too much; still it's clear that he plays a part in the general design. Sara thus is lower class, the nester woman, with physical knowledge, who lives in the present and expresses her wisdom by folk sayings. Wilcher is upper middle class, the conserver, with social and historical knowledge, who directs towards the past and who expresses his wisdom through his brother's ironic verses. Gulley is class-less (having left the middle class for the anomalous position of artist), the creator-destroyer, with metaphysical knowledge, who directs towards the future and who expresses his wisdom through Blake's verses.[28]

Now, although these three are clearly opposed to each other, the scheme into which they fit makes itself obviously felt as an inclusive one, in which the different individual parts find their proper places, and the form of the trilogy thus is a form of acceptance which accounts in part for the nearly total absence of the pattern of invasion which characterized the early works. Those invasions which do remain have an entirely changed effect and fit into the pattern of acceptance. The major invading force in the trilogy is Gulley, the most dynamic of the characters, who can be said to invade the Monday home, Wilcher's house, and the Hickson residence. But in each case the relationship becomes a positive one. The relationship between Monday and Jimson is never really worked out, though to the end Monday thinks of Gulley as a great artist; but Gulley's invasion of Wilcher's house, though seemingly full of conflict, is resolved into a financial arrangement by which Gulley gets twenty-two shillings, sixpence a week (185–86 *HM*). The conflict with Hickson is a major one in the sense that Gulley is drawn to it again and again—and of course the relationship between artist and patron is a major part of the artist theme—but nevertheless when Hickson dies, Gulley cries for him and tells Coker, "I've had a blow. I've lost my oldest friend" (247 *HM*).[29]

Seen in this way, Gulley's many conflicts appear not to consist of forces which fully oppose each other. His continuing opposition to Sara is really a complementary one, and this includes the blows he gave her while married and the final blow which kills her. The relationship is summarized in a paragraph which uses Blake: "As Billy would say, through generation into regeneration. Materiality, that is, Sara, the old female nature, having attempted to button up the prophetic spirit, that is to say, Gulley Jimson, in her placket-hole, got a bonk on the conk, and was reduced to her proper status, as spiritual fodder" (52 *HM*). In fact, the two are constantly inspiriting each other. The relationship between Gulley and Hickson is actually a complementary one also, in its way, and Gulley says with only a little irony, "I think he's [Hickson's] been a good friend to English art" (107 *HM*). Similarly, the destruction of the wall which contains Gulley's Creation by the bulldozer of the City council is also accepted, though with a great deal more of irony, as "a resolute act of anti-aggression" (296 *HM*).

In *To Be a Pilgrim,* the invasion of the beautiful saloon at Tolbrook—metaphor for everything traditional and beautiful to Wilcher—is similarly accepted. "The very ruin of this beautiful room is become a part of my happiness. I say no longer 'Change must come, and this change, so bitter to me, is a necessary ransom for what I keep.' I have surrendered because I cannot fight and now it seems to me that not change but life itself has lifted me and mine forward on the stream" (328 *TB P*).

Additional examples of what in the early books were invasions and full confrontations but which are developed here as accepted juxtapositions further abound in the trilogy. Wilcher's experience of invasion, when he addresses the wrong group during his brother's political campaign and is roughed up, is turned simply into a ridiculous incident which shows something of the nature of political campaigning and more of Wilcher's incapability (157 *TB P*). It has nothing of the feeling of the clash of forces in the other works. Again, Sara and Rozzie, who actually are rivals for Gulley (though Sara is not aware of it at the time) and who are opposite in temperament, are close friends. And Gulley, who sees them as opposite, sees them also as complementary:

> Rozzie had a conscience; Sara had a purpose and an object in life. Rozzie was a God-fearing heathen that never went to church in case of what might happen to her there; Sara was a God-using Christian that went to church to please herself and pick up some useful ideas about religion, hats and the local gossip.
>
> Sara was a shot in the arm; she brought you alive one way or another; the very idea of Sara could always make me swear or jump or dance or sweat. Because of her damned independence and hypocrisy. When you knew Sara, you knew womankind, and no one who doesn't know womankind knows anything of Nature. But Rozzie was only female and she never stirred up anything but love and pity. Sara was a menace and a tonic, my best enemy; Rozzie was a disease, my worst friend. Sara made a man of me and damn nearly a murderer; Rozzie might have turned me into a lop-eared crooner (254 *HM*).

Presumably this desire to emphasize acceptance and inclusion is also the reason why the two men of the trilogy are not personally directly opposed, as, say, Hickson and Gulley might have been. Though Hickson and Gulley are also part of the same pattern, still their personal opposition might have made the confrontation more direct than was desirable in this complementary, juxtaposing trilogy.

Indeed the three main characters have as much to unify them as to divide them. Perhaps the most amusing connection between Wilcher and Gulley is their common desire to hit Sara. Gulley actually does it. Wilcher only thinks about it, but it is the nose he is thinking of hitting (322 *TB P*).

They are all three nonconformists, basically symbolists, for whom the material world is only a door to the true world of the spirit. Gulley is a thoroughgoing and conscious symbolist. Sara, however, while she gets a great deal of enjoyment out of her body and out of the goods of the world, is just what Gulley says of her: she is an Eve, "That falls every night to rise in the morning. And wonder at herself. Knowing everything and still surprised. Living in innocence" (41–42 *HM*).

Wilcher responds to the same quality in her, and it is no less convincing that he exaggerates it over the sensual joys which she also gives him. As for himself, Wilcher repeatedly finds himself trapped by the material things he so loves, since what he considers truly significant is the life of the spirit. Tolbrook seems to him in one image to be a coffin imprisoning his spirit: "The walls closed in; the roof came down upon me. The house became a coffin and it seemed that I had been shut up alive." And his final vision mediates between the body and the spirit: "What is material? What is the body? Is not this house the house of spirits, made by generations of lovers? I touched in my mother the warmth of a love that did not belong to either of us. Why should I not feel, when I lie in English ground, the passion of a spirit that beats in all English souls?" (342 *TB P*).

In addition, all three are also thoroughgoing sinners when judged by ordinary standards, though they are guiltless on their own terms. And all three end their works with a thoroughgoing acceptance of life as it is.

The difference between the earlier and later works can be seen again by comparing the position of women in several of them. Sara in the first trilogy and Nina in the second are both unifying elements who tie together the other two characters and relate them to each other. As such they serve on the one hand as examples of the eternal feminine character which finds its specific expression in different ways at different times, and on the other as structural elements helping to juxtapose two opposing types. It is because of Sara that Wilcher and Gulley meet, and because of Nina that Nimmo and Latter have anything to do with each other. The three characters then are examples of types which are fundamental and which together represent varying parts of one single total sociological situation, and of human typology.

Bamu in *Mister Johnson* is also an eternal human type—as her similarity to Mrs. Rudbeck indicates—but her role in the book is not to relate but rather to contrast with Mr. Johnson's dynamic quality. She represents, in short, one of the forces which makes up the sociological situation in which Johnson lives. Married to him, she also puts psychological pressure on him, but what we watch is the way Johnson relates to her. She represents a force, and helps to show the forces acting on the main character.

Even more clearly, Osi in *The African Witch* represents the elemental life force which all humans are subject to and, more specifically, the irrational ju-ju element which works so strongly on Aladai and causes his disaster. Elizabeth, on the other hand, represents another kind of feminine force. Suggesting also the archetypal female goddess, she is primarily a feminine version of the rational conservative.

In *An American Visitor,* again, Marie is opposed to Bewsher; she represents another of the forces acting on the total African situation, the fundamentalist-nonconformist impulse towards anarchy. And even Mrs. Carr in *Aissa Saved* serves to stand in opposition to her husband's rational religion. Each of these women represents one force opposing others. Nina and Sara connect.

## III

The juxtaposing form of the trilogies, especially the first trilogy, has fundamentally a comic effect, especially when seen in terms of the discussion of comedy in Northrop Frye's *Anatomy of Criticism*. In developing his outline of comedy as a pattern of inclusion, Frye presents a handy description of New Comedy: "a young man wants a young woman . . . his desire is resisted by some opposition, usually paternal, and . . . near the end of the play some twist in the plot enables the hero to have his will." [30]

Frye also describes the major character types. There is the young woman who tends to have few individual characteristics. There is the blocking character of the action, the *senex,* an older figure who in one way or another occupies a position of power in the society. Typically, the victory over him by the young hero implies a criticism of the social structure which has allowed him to amass his power, whether it is money or another form of the goods valued by society. This man is also ordinarily an *alazon,* an impostor, and he is opposed in the structure of the comedy by the *eiron,* a self-deprecating type; the most typical relation between these two, the *agon,* is seen in "the multitude of comic scenes in which one character soliloquizes while another makes sarcastic asides to the audience. . . ." A third basic character is the *bomolochos,* the buffoon whose "function is to increase the mood of festivity rather than contribute to the plot." [31]

Gulley Jimson himself fits three of the four major comic types; that is, he is *alazon, eiron,* and *bomolochos* all in one. Indeed, the typical method of his discussions with himself is essentially the *agon* between *alazon* and *eiron.* This was noted earlier as the pattern which makes him correct his own exaggerations, deflate his own pretences, and contrasts his state of need with his pretended success as a bourgeois. And by Sara's evidence, if no other, Gulley certainly fills the function of the *bomolochos,* which is to "increase the mood of festivity."

There is something of the *alazon,* the pretender, both in Sara and in Wilcher as well. As already noted, when Sara sees herself for the first time, on her honeymoon in Paris, in a mirror, she can't recognize herself; she looks to herself like a common country trollop made up to look like a belle. The scene suggests the title of her book, *Herself Surprised,* and the element of ignorance and discovery about herself which is so fundamental to her character, even if it is not her most outstanding characteristic. Not only does Wilcher dress up as an Indian, but there is a more serious and typical pretence in his desire to be a missionary. Furthermore he continually imitates his brother Edward and his sister Lucy. Indeed, his commitment to a life of things brings up the question of identity in a way which cannot be ultimately solved. In a sense, whatever a man like Wilcher does, he is a pretender, an *alazon,* and his success in the terms of his society, as a rich man, a

sober man, a staid conserver of things and law, is contra-
dicted by his acts in old age which deny value to his previous
life. He burns down one house, threatens to burn down another, and exposes himself to young girls.

Beyond the individual characters, the movement of the
entire trilogy can be seen as fitting into the pattern of the
comedy described by Frye. Gulley, in this sense, is the young
man; and he is repeatedly described by Sara as young. He is
after the girl, but she is Sara only in one sense. In a more
meaningful sense he is after the essence of Sara, her quality
as Eve. This is the same quality which he also sees in the
cat in the bar scene just before his last stroke. "And no one
is more kind than a cat. Her own kind," Gulley says, emphasizing in the pun the natural individuality of the cat (279
*HM*). Following Blake's terminology he also sees aesthetic insight as the "maiden." [32] But aesthetic insight comes from
being directly in touch with the essence of reality, and when
his picture turns out badly he thinks it might be the "result
of losing touch with the real Makay" (43 *HM*).

Gulley's quest for essential reality is of course a personal
one, a subjective, internal search, which has no direct relationship to social success or the approval of society. Still, there
is a marginal relationship, enough in any case to make Gulley's rejection by society a significant element in the work,
aside even from the difficulties he has finding enough money,
food, paint, brushes, canvas, and such to be able to continue
to paint. And, if the "maiden" Gulley is after is personified
in Sara, then the social obstacle, the enemy to his achievement is personified in Wilcher, who thus acts the part of the
*senex* in the comedy.

That Wilcher is in his own way after the "maiden" and
discovers her at the end of his life, that Gulley is also the
*alazon* who insists on denying himself success while he is
grasping for it, that Sara is the enemy of the artistic impulse
while she functions as the embodiment of the creative
"maiden"—all these are complicating elements, typical of
Cary's ironic vision. The basic framework, however, is clear.[33]

Frye himself mentions Gulley Jimson as an example of

a tragic pattern of exclusion in which there is an ironic reversal of values. Describing what he calls "low mimetic tragedy," Frye says it has at its basis pathos, "The root idea of [which] is the exclusion of an individual on our level from a social group to which he is trying to belong." [34] *The Horse's Mouth,* Frye says, belongs to a special branch of this type— including also such works as *The Idiot* and *The Good Soldier Schweik*—which produces "an ironic deadlock in which the hero is regarded as a fool or worse by the fictional society, and yet impresses the real audience as having something more valuable than his society has." [35] Frye's insight here is shrewd and suggestive but seems to be limited only to *The Horse's Mouth* as a single work. In terms of the trilogy as a whole, the comic pattern appears more clearly. "The tendency of comedy," Frye says, "is to include as many people as possible in its final society: the blocking characters are more often reconciled or converted than simply repudiated." [36] Here the blocking character, Wilcher, is in fact reconciled and fits himself into the same pattern as Gulley. Frye also describes the movement of comedy "from a society controlled by habit, ritual, bondage, arbitrary law and the older characters to a society controlled by youth and pragmatic freedom . . . a movement from illusion to reality." [37] This comment, too, seems to apply directly to the trilogy, where all three characters move from the material behind the universe to the spiritual truth, and to acceptance of life as it is, freed as far as each character is capable of it, from "habit, ritual, bondage, and arbitrary law."

The same comment applies also, perhaps even more directly, to the African books, especially to *Mister Johnson* where the basic opposition is between habit and pragmatic freedom, between Johnson and Ajali, between Johnson and the habit-filled world of Bamu and her family, between Johnson's clear vision and Celia's inability to see Africa. In *The African Witch* the point is made perhaps excessively clear when Rackham contrasts Aladai with Honeywood on the basis of their freedom:

> Aladai was worth six Honeywoods, both as a man and an intelligence; he was worth an infinitude of Honeywoods, because Honeywood was a robot, a set of reactions, a creature ruled entirely by prejudice and a mass of contradictory impulses and inhibitions, which he called his opinions, and thought of as his character. He was a wooden man danced on strings; and anyone could make him tick (192–93 *Af W*).

This conflict—a part of Cary's interest in freedom—constantly makes Cary appose the free man to the creature of habit and law. Most typically, the free man loses the contest, in the sense that he pays with his life, but wins in the sense, described by Frye, that the reader considers his way as more valuable.

On the whole, a greater measure of victory tends to go to the free men in the later works than in the earlier. Aissa, Bewsher, Aladai—all three freer, less creatures of habit and of law than those they live among—all die, without seeming to effect a great deal. Their value in social terms, that is, outside of the purely personal terms which give them the dynamic quality that makes them stand out is questionable. Johnson, however, measurably affects Rudbeck, minor member of the British administration though he may be, and Gulley's kind of spiritual freedom is the standard one of the trilogy.

The second trilogy has the form of comedy also, in a way which is both clearer than the first and more ironically different. On the surface of things, Jim Latter seems to be the young man who loves the girl, Nina, and who is stopped from getting her by the *senex*, Chester Nimmo, who marries Nina. Eventually, Nina divorces Nimmo, and Latter and Nina marry. The major complicating factor is that Latter, the young hero, who is prevented from getting the girl because he has insufficient money, by an older man who has social power not quite honestly gotten, is actually a less free man than his opponent. Moreover, the older man sees himself—with some justification—as the young hero who is prevented by the social class of his bride and her relations from truly winning her. It is this work in which the free man reaches his highest success—judged from the point of view of both society and of aesthetic form—but it is also this work in which it is hardest to disentangle from the free man the element of the *senex*. There is no question that Nimmo is the freest of the characters, but in his formal role he is not at all *eiron* but all *alazon*, which is why Nina's son can build a successful nightclub act around an imitation of him. Curiously, the role of *eiron* here is given not to his opponent, Jim Latter, but rather to the girl, Nina, who deflates him effectively but with great sympathy. It is also in this work that the *agon* is least definitive in its conclusion, with the girl remaining at the end, as throughout the books, torn between the two men and at the same time loyal to both. While this conclusion has gained for the second trilogy a major attack as being indeterminate,[38] in terms of the comic mythos described by Frye the three books are surely the most inclusive of Cary's works.

It achieves this inclusiveness by eliminating from the comic form the element of *pharmakos* (the scapegoat) entirely. This *pharmakos* element is strong in Cary's early work, where Aissa and Aladai are overtly scapegoat types whose exclusion has something to do with their excessive vitality. Johnson, like Gulley, fits into the ironic pattern associated with the *pharmakos*, whom Frye describes as "guilty in the sense that he is a member of a guilty society, or living in a world where such injustices are an inescapable part of existence." [39] Johnson's exclusion from his society still suggests that there exists some kind of value system, even though the system which rejects Johnson and Gulley from full participation is not a proper one. In the second trilogy there is no *pharmakos*, even though Jim Latter tries to insist on a closed off system which will make scapegoats out of all three characters. On the contrary, the system which the trilogy as a whole insists on is an open one, in which everyone has his place, so much so that it is virtually impossible to separate the young hero from the old blocking character, both being equally virtuous and equally sinful, and above all equally necessary to the social and spiritual reality.

# *Notes*

1 *The African Witch* was first published in 1936. It is accurately described by Bloom as "Cary's largest, most comprehensive African novel." *The Indeterminate World*, p. 52.

2 Cary confesses to having shared this view when he first joined the African Service, and he describes it explicitly: there are "officials of high standing and long African experience, who say, 'I knew such and such a tribe when they were bare-arsed pagans, the finest chaps I ever met, honest as the day, straight as their backs, clean as their own rain-washed skins. And look at them now since they got stores and ploughs and mission schools, trousers and clap. The lousiest, laziest, most worthless lot of mean bums that ever transfigured the dung-heap they live in.'" *The Case for African Freedom and other Writings on Africa* (Austin: University of Texas Press, 1962), pp. 37–38, hereafter abbreviated as *Case*.

3 In his article, "Fiction and the 'Matrix of Analogy,'" *Kenyon Review*, IX (1949), 539–60, Mark Schorer demonstrates how an examination of the metaphorical quality of language can lead to insights into the theme, form, structure and style of a novel. There is no attempt to imitate that brilliant demonstration here. On the whole, Cary's language leads most directly to an exposition of character, especially in the trilogies where Cary speaks determinedly in the voices of his creations. The invasions and confrontations are less a matter demonstrable by language than by the larger shape of the plot.

4 See, for instance, Mahood, p. 169: "*Mister Johnson*, the best of Cary's African novels and considered by many people (including at one time its author) to be his best novel. . . ." and Arnold Kettle, *An Introduction to the English Novel* (London: Hutchinson University Library, 1953), Vol. 2, p. 179: "I do not see how within its appointed limits *Mister Johnson* could be better done."

5 Perhaps because she is the kind of character often described by reviewers as "larger than life," Elizabeth has brought more than one reader to grief. Andrew Wright, apparently confusing her with Coker, calls her a "spellbinder," whose power for good and evil depends on her "rhetorical skill." *Joyce Cary*, p. 60.
Bloom on the other hand calls her "a figure of darkness and murderous ignorance." He compounds his error by saying that Aladai "sinks into the most brutal savagery." *Indeterminate World*, p. 54. There is in fact no mention of any brutal or savage act by Aladai, other than his unsuccessful rebellion, to which neither adjective really applies. He *is* present at a brutal and savage meeting where his will and intellect are made ineffective by Coker's rhetoric, but that is something else again.

6 Mahood sees this doubling as a failure for Cary, who was unable "to get his character into focus," p. 63.

7 Cf. Cary in his pamphlet, *Britain and West Africa:* "A political crisis, however caused, does not please Provincial Residents and Governors. It does not assist District Officers in their careers." *Case,* p. 185.

8 As Mahood shows, the two were intended to be parallels, both caught in the same conflict between the captive and the free. See pp. 145–66, esp. her citation of a note by Cary: "Aladai behaves bravely, coolly strung up. *Just like Rackham,*" p. 152.

It is one of Mahood's main points that the opposition between control and surrender is Cary's theme in each of his first three books.

9 The name Dryas carries the suggestion primarily of the intuitive, physical, desirable nymph, although it may also bear the implication of "dry." In the same way, Coote suggests primarily the strange, but may also call to mind the grace of the bird.

10 See Cary's Preface to the Carfax edition, pp. 9, 11. For Aladai's nationalism cf. Cary's discussion of the topic in *Power in Men* (Seattle: University of Washington Press, 1963), pp. 168–69.

11 Douglas Grant, "The Novel and its Critical Terms," *Essays in Criticism,* 1 (1951), 428. Grant's more general point about plot, that the modern novel contains little action because it sees the modern character as victim rather than actor, obviously does not apply directly to Cary. Cf. Edward Case's interesting ideological essay praising Cary for showing man as able to act freely. See, "The Free World of Joyce Cary," *Modern Age,* III (1959), 115–24.

12 Education is, as a matter of fact, a major theme in this book, and there is hardly a Cary novel in which the topic does not come up. *The African Witch* ends with two not very successful students: Akande Tom, who stops his studies before he begins, and a native sergeant, who gives a comic exhibition of his reading skill.

13 The historical background of indirect rule is neatly given by Mahood; see esp. pp. 6, 65–68. On the same subject see Christopher Fyfe, "The Colonial Situation in *Mister Johnson,*" *Modern Fiction Studies,* IX (1963), 226–30.

14 The term is Cottee's (234 *Am V*).

15 Mahood comments that Cary contains "a seam of Old Coaster yarns which sometimes mar the earlier novels with meaningless horror and violence," p. 169. Cary was himself certainly aware of this, perhaps excessive, coarseness. In his Preface to the Carfax edition of *The African Witch,* p. 11, he says that Africa "demands a certain kind of story, a certain violence and coarseness of detail, almost a fabulous treatment to keep it in its place."

16 The first trilogy includes *Herself Surprised,* 1941, *To Be a Pilgrim,* 1942, and *The Horse's Mouth,* 1944. The second trilogy includes *Prisoner of Grace,* 1952, *Except The Lord,* 1953, and *Not Honour More,* 1955.

17 Of the three British novelists known for their postwar serial novels, only Lawrence Durrell in the *Alexandria Quartet* has tried for anything like Cary's complexity. Anthony Powell's *Music of Time* series and C. P. Snow's *Strangers and Brothers* series are simply sequential.

[18] Charles G. Hoffman, who calls Cary's trilogies a major development in the multiple novel, points out that Cary conceived of the trilogy at first as a "triptych," with each panel throwing light on the others. See *Joyce Cary: The Comedy of Freedom* (University of Pittsburgh Press, 1964), p. 4. It is also clear in Hoffman that while Cary was interested in the multiple form very early—see *ibid.*, p. 18—his idea of the trilogy as an including, juxtaposing form took him some time to develop. His earlier notion of the trilogy was of a form which would help give the true facts of history, apparently in the sociological way of *Castle Corner.* See "The Genesis and Development of Joyce Cary's First Trilogy," *PMLA*, LXXVIII (1963), 432.

[19] For Cary's interest in character types see Wright, Chapter 3, "The World as Character," pp. 72–106. For the types in the first trilogy, see Fred Stockholder, "The Triple Vision in Joyce Cary's First Trilogy," *Modern Fiction Studies*, IX (1963), 276–83, and Hazard Adams, "Joyce Cary's Three Speakers," *Modern Fiction Studies*, V (1959), 108–20. For the Blake parallels see Adams, "Blake and Gulley Jimson: English Symbolists," *Critique*, III (1959), 3–14.

[20] Defoe's books are probably the best known of this tradition, though it extends far beyond, including much of the Newgate literature, a great deal of the picaresque, and the bulk of the stories in such ladies' magazines as *True Confessions.*

[21] Hazard Adams disagrees with this view. In arguing that Wilcher never accepts the future because he sees it only in terms of Sara, who is the past for him, Adams seems, however, to overlook this ending, and Wilcher's entire relationship to his nephew and niece, Bobby and Ann. "Three Speakers," p. 109.

[22] Cary uses a similar metaphor to emphasize the "determined" nature of the physical world: "What would happen to liberty . . . if a cricketer's bat suddenly turned into cotton-wool or an engineer's bridge suddenly turned into macaroni?" *Power in Men*, p. 254.

[23] There may also be a sadistic element in Gulley's violence. If so, it would be another complementary contrast to Wilcher who was certainly seen by Cary as masochistic. See Cary's notes for the trilogy as quoted in Hoffman, "Genesis and Development," p. 437.

[24] It has been suggested that Gulley's diction is similar to Joyce's verbal richness in *Ulysses*. This suggestion overlooks the fact that Gulley's language is used primarily to characterize him. Sara speaks one way, Wilcher another, and Gulley a third. The richness of the language does not, as it does primarily in Joyce, establish a pattern of symbolic interconnections.

This cavil is certainly not, however, meant to deny a possible influence of Joyce on Cary. He may well have been thinking of Joyce's language when he developed Gulley's diction, even if he did use it for another purpose. He may also have thought of Joyce's use of myth as a framework for a modern novel when he decided to base *The Horse's Mouth* on Blake's thesis. Such speculation will have to wait for substantiation until a full biography of Cary is written, or until his letters or notebooks are published.

25 As James Hall points out in his *The Tragic Comedians: Seven Modern British Novelists* (Bloomington: Indiana University Press, 1963), p. 95, the destructive and creative impulses are inseparable in the whale's smile.

The creation of works of art which exist only briefly has interestingly enough become increasingly usual in contemporary art under the name of "Happenings." On at least one occasion the happening turned out to be the destruction of a kind of sculpture. See Calvin Tomkins' profile of Jean Tinguely, "Beyond the Machine," *New Yorker*, XXXVII (February 10, 1962), 44–93.

26 The description is also partly the result of her formal place in the book, to typify the unreal quality of Beulah.

27 The phallic implications of this comment about the serpent are never discussed in *The Horse's Mouth*, nor is any sexual element of Gulley's work—aside from Coker's prudish objections to nudity—though all three of his paintings are extremely open to such considerations.

28 Cary certainly intended the class differences to be clear. See his note, quoted in Hoffman, "Genesis and Development," p. 135: "Sara then offered herself as a good person to shew a womans [sic] point of view; also that of a class dependent on events without much power to understand them; Wilcher well educated & connected, was to give that of an upper middle class man, close to political sources; and Gulley, that of the artist, with a completely different angle from either of them."

This note also makes it clear that Wilcher was to give the standard social-historical view, while Sara was to give the personal view. Not mentioned here, but obviously intended, was a philosophical emphasis in *The Horse's Mouth*, the book which spends a great deal of its force defeating Spinoza by using Blake's arguments.

29 Gulley is sympathetic to deaths. He visits Rozzie's grave regularly, though he naturally takes the opportunity to make a little something on the flowers he leaves at her grave. He also sympathizes with Sara's concern for a proper burial.

The real concern with death in the trilogy, however, belongs to Wilcher, who details the deaths of all the major characters in his book, Edward's, Lucy's, Bill's, Amy's, his father's. This is partly because he is close to death himself, partly because it is his nature to look back, partly because he lived so much in others that their deaths are of major significance to him.

30 Northrop Frye, *Anatomy of Criticism: Four Essays* (Princeton University Press, 1957), p. 163.

31 For the full discussion in Frye, see pp. 163–86. A fourth type of comic character, the *agroikos,* is a churlish buffoon who sometimes acts as straight man and who in one way or another interrupts the festivities crudely, "a kill-joy who tries to stop the fun." The *agroikos* does not figure significantly in the trilogies, though Jim Latter has affinities with him and Coker pretends to be of the type also.

32 In two examples of this usage, Gulley says: "I didn't know if I was after a real girl or a succubus in the shape of a fairy," and, "The maiden

fled away so fast that he [Cezanne] hardly caught her once a year" (64–65 *HM*).

33 Placing the characters in such a framework is meant to add to the common view that Gulley and Sara are picaresque characters, not to deny it. Robert Alter, for instance, in his study of the picaresque, says that Gulley "embodies the distinctive heroism and hedonism of the picaresque anti-heroic attitude." *Rogue's Progress: Studies in the Picaresque Novel* (Cambridge: Harvard University Press, 1964), p. 132. In this view, Alter seems to be overlooking the other side of Gulley, who after all takes seriously his art, himself, and his fight with society. Similarly, placing Sara in the more bourgeois tradition of Moll Flanders (as e.g., by Adams, "Three Speakers," p. 110, and by Wright, *Joyce Cary,* pp. 111–12) ignores her meaning for Gulley.

34 *Anatomy of Criticism,* p. 39.

35 *Ibid.,* p. 48.

36 *Ibid.,* p. 165.

37 *Loc. cit.*

38 Bloom objects to all of Cary's work as being indeterminate but he reserves his special attack for the second trilogy.

39 *Anatomy,* p. 41. It ought perhaps to be added here that the *pharmakos* can exist either in comedy or in tragedy. Indeed in Frye's system, comedy as a mythos is not antithetical to tragedy but a part of the same general pattern.

# 2. Points of View

I

The change in Cary's plot structure is accompanied by a parallel change in his use of the point of view. The earlier African works—in which the opposition is comparatively direct, the themes comparatively schematic, the tone comparatively melodramatic, the interest comparatively sociological —have a teeming multiplicity of point of view, alternating rapidly from character to character. The later trilogies—more indirectly juxtaposed, more humanly fleshed out, more comic —rigidly limit the point of view to one character per book.[1]

An examination of the point of view in Cary is extremely useful, but in order to get into the essence of his fiction it is necessary to look at the matter in a more substantive way than is usual. Ordinarily the point of view is considered as a technical device which adds verisimilitude and which has basically a formal and psychological effect.[2] Another way to look at point of view is to consider its effect on the total statement of the work. Thus, the omniscience of Fielding's point of view in *Tom Jones* helps to suggest that the universe is orderly, knowable if not known, and that there exists in nature a pattern for a perfect human order. In the same way, the absence of the narrator as a felt character in Virginia Woolf helps to suggest the opposite—that only a subjective reality exists.[3]

In Cary's case, the multiplicity of point of view helps to suggest a multiplicity of standards, a variety of ways of life, each one accepted from within the point of view which bears the authority of the narrator at any given time.[4] The effect is loosely similar to the one which Erich Auerbach calls attention to in Homer, in his brilliant comparison between the representational technique of the Homeric and the Biblical mimesis.[5] In his discussion of the *Odyssey,* Auerbach stops at Homer's shift in the narration away from the adventures of Odysseus in order to detail the origin of the scar which his old nurse Eurycleia recognizes, and which may reveal his identity too soon. This kind of "excursus" from the main story during a critical moment is similar to many other interruptions which allow Homer to describe a character or an object just introduced into the narrative. In part because of such unhurried shifts in the narration, Auerbach characterizes the Homeric style as one of "fully externalized description, uniform illumination, uninterrupted connection, free expression, all events in the foreground, displaying unmistakable meanings, few elements of historical development and of psychological perspective." [6]

Not specifically mentioned by Auerbach, but certainly fitting into the very pattern he has described, are the many times Homer shifts away from the narrative line of the moment to anticipate what is going to occur to his main characters and to prepare the way for them. One example is the arrival of Telemachus at Pylos, the home of Nestor, at the beginning of Book III. The story has been following Telemachus, and Book II ends with Telemachus sailing on his ship to find news of his father after having (with the help of Athene) cleverly outwitted the suitors. His stop with Nestor is the subject of Book III, and the opening paragraph of the book shifts its view away from Telemachus to the visited, who are busy sacrificing to Poseidon. Rieu's translation shows the scene: "There were nine companies in session, with five hundred men in each, and every company had nine bulls to offer. They had just tasted the victims' entrails and were burning the pieces from the thighs in the god's honour as the trim ship came bearing down upon them." [7] As the last phrase indicates, the view has shifted away from the ship to the shore, so that the reader is now, as it were, with Nestor and his company ready to welcome Telemachus.

Again in the lovely Nausicaa incident the shift away from Odysseus lying exhausted on the Phaeacian beach to Nausicaa gives a full view of her maidenliness so that when the two finally do meet, the reader can understand fully the implication of this confrontation of—in Homer's metaphor—the mountain lion and the gentle deer.

This shifting of the viewpoint—similar, in fact, to the shifts in Cary—has as both its cause and effect an acceptance of reality on its own terms. As Auerbach says, "And this real world into which we are lured, exists for itself, contains nothing but itself; the Homeric poems conceal nothing, they contain no teaching and no secret second meaning. Homer can be analyzed . . . but he cannot be interpreted." [8]

In Cary, too, the shifting of the point of view produces narratives in which all aspects of reality are accepted on their own terms, and in which any one element of the world is as knowable as any other. To use Auerbach's terms again, the narrative has uniform illumination and every incident is in the foreground. The major difference is that while in Homer the effect produces a sense of social and moral unity, in Cary it produces an acceptance of different social systems and different approaches to life. When Homer, for example, shifts to Nausicaa to show her difference from Odysseus, and thus prepares for what might be the shock of the meeting, he does so primarily because Nausicaa and Odysseus are both cultured human beings who fit into the only worthy pattern of life, and his knowledge of the proper rhetorical and social skills and her superior social grace will overcome the shock. In Cary, the shifts emphasize the difference in fundamental attitudes, say, between the pagans of Kolu and the Christian converts of the Carrs, while accepting both groups as perfectly normal within their own points of view.

The matter is complicated by three separate levels in the point of view. There is, first, the momentary view which focuses on the specific individuals or groups, and which suggests strongly that the standards of each are valid. There is, second, the sense of multiplicity produced by the frequent shifts, suggesting that all standards are valid only subjectively and strongly indicating that conflict is unavoidable. But there is also a third view, which encompasses them all, and this is given by the implied narrator who controls the viewpoints, the one who actually does the shifting, the consciousness which in the trilogies points to the many connections between the various books. This last level suggests very strongly that there is a single, external, objective reality within which the individual groups find their relative place, and that there is a single pattern of human behavior which subsumes all individual and social differences.

Curiously, as if to match these levels of the point of view, the narration speaks not with a single voice but rather with three different voices. The first voice is that of a knowledgeable tourist guide or newspaper reporter. He has superficial kinds of historical information, and his knowledgeability gives the same sense of social and political reality which newspapers provide. The second voice is that of an observer who sees and hears. He is a camera and recording machine without insight and without human reaction. His information gives a sense of the physical reality. The third voice is that of the narrator who knows all, when necessary. At times he speaks with the assurance and authority associated with the traditional omniscient author. His information provides psychological and philosophical reality.

Cary's first book, *Aissa Saved*, opens with the first voice, placing the situation in a formal, official, historical context:

> Shibi Rest Camp on the Niger was built by Bradgate, then assistant resident, about 1912. He wanted to make his station there, but the doctors refused to pass the site on account of the swamps close behind which fill it with mosquitoes.
>
> Afterwards the Winkworth Memorial Mission obtained leave to use the buildings and added to them a chapel and hospital (13 *AS*).[9]

This narrating tone belongs to a Britisher, since he can describe the Christian natives during their argument over whether to go to Kolu as "quite as angry and obstinate as those of a Sunday School at home" (17 *AS*). He is also rather dull, and it is likely that he is himself quite unaware of the irony in the opening which allows missionaries to build a hospital on a site which the doctors would not pass for a station.

This same narrative tone is used to open the second section of the book which describes Kolu, the town about to be invaded.

> Kolu was crowded for the feast on account of a religious revival. The drought and bad prices of 1921 which followed the boom years of the war hurt the pagans, who were farmers, much more than the Mahomedan tradesmen . . . (30 *AS*).

In this case, however, the voice soon becomes one belonging to a pagan native. At least it is a voice which supports the pagan chief when the chief refuses to accept either Bradgate's explanation that the slump was due to war and the drought, or the emir's explanation that it was due to God's will:

> But these statements were obviously absurd. As a pagan chief said: "This white man does not know anything about our country and the Emir is tired and does not care about anything . . ." (30 *AS*).

Similarly, the voice supports the arguments of the priest Owule who explains that the bad times were due to the dissatisfaction of the goddess Oke: "his denunciations and appeals were confirmed by Oke herself" (31 *AS*).

The careful limit placed on the narrator's knowledge here makes possible much of the irony which runs throughout this and the other early Cary works. It is, for instance, because the view is strictly held to the pagans that the reader also accepts their evaluation of the fearless undignified headman, Musa, and thus is able to see the irony of Musa's dismissal by the Carrs, each sending him away for a different reason (44 *AS*).

Irony is also often the effect of the second voice, that of

the narrator who gives purely physical descriptions, often of objects and scenes, but most typically of human actions, as if their only dimension is one of action, totally without any motivation or inner content. For instance, this voice describes an argument between the native Christians purely in terms of physical action: "Immediately Nagulo threw himself at him, Salé, who agreed with Frederick, caught hold of Nagulo, Aissa beat Salé, and Salé abused Aditutu. Screams and roars were heard, like the battle cries of lions and stallions" (17 *AS*).

The effect in context is far from being mock epic, in spite of the reference to lions and stallions. On the other hand, the purely physical level of the description makes possible the irony (perhaps the excessively cheap irony) of the sentence which follows: "The discussion of this point was always animated . . . " (17 *AS*).

Quite aside from such incidental ironies, however, this voice is basic to Cary. It allows him to show characters as acting without having to give their traditional motivation at the same time. This certainly does not mean that he sees them as unmotivated, or that he is not interested in their motivations. It simply allows him to divide the physical action from the inner state to which it is connected. He does this partly so as to emphasize his belief that people act more often without realizing exactly what they are doing rather than acting after an intelligent weighing of the issues. Partly, too, he does it to emphasize that action often comes in his best characters as an immediate translation of their feelings, without the intervention of the intellect. On occasion he does it for psychological verisimilitude, to show the effect of one man's actions on another man, or group of men, who are totally unaware of his motivation. Always the voice focuses attention on the action itself.

The matter is especially significant in such characters as Johnson, whose peculiar individuality is developed precisely because his purely physical acts, first seen by themselves, can then be connected to his divided situation. As a result Johnson gets a double existence: he is both a poet in action who transforms his feelings directly into action, as well as an isolated figure whose actions are ridiculous in the social context.

Here the nature of Aissa, and the basic problem of the book, requires a somewhat similar treatment. Aissa is an extremely vital person, vigorous and dynamic in all her actions. As in other Cary characters, none of her actions is limited by common sense, and she fights for those she loves with excessive abandon: "She was the sort of girl who could not take advice and could not control herself like a sensible creature" (46 *AS*).[10] In addition, she is unable "to hide her feelings" (47 *AS*), but is always acting in immediate reaction to them. It is thus quite in order for Cary to describe her actions primarily in physical terms. When she is among the native Christians who have gone to Kolu and are singing hymns, "she rolled her head and eyes in most mournful fashion, raised her flat nose to the sky and opened and shut her big Cupid's mouth like a fish drinking" (49 *AS*). The ostensible reason for her contortions is that the hymn is a mournful one and that she is, as usual, acting out her emotions with extravagance.

There is more involved. The hymn she is singing translates as:

> All things I like best
> I sacrifice to His blood (49 *AS*).

It is the same hymn she sings at the end of the book when in order to provide the rain which the community needs she, in a frenzy of renewed faith, literally sacrifices "all things I like best," including her son Abba. The manner of her giving her son at that time is basically not different from her excessive expression during the singing of the hymn. At that time, too, she acts out her spiritual exaltation directly and with what is certainly extravagance according to common sense standards. Throughout, the physical description focuses attention on her actions and thus on the quality of her sacrifice, in which lies the basic theme of the book.

Her sacrifice is contrasted to that of two others. Similar

to her immediate, nonrational expression of faith is that of
Mrs. Carr, who wins over her husband to the first trip to
Kolu, just as Aissa wins over Ojo, who believes, rationally,
that human sacrifice is ju-ju. The descriptions of the two
conversions are very similar: Ojo "had called them [Aissa and
another convert, Makoto] pagans because of their pagan
rites—but their hearts were more Christian than his. He was
fighting against the very spirit of love and sacrifice, against
the wisdom of Jesus and the power of the Holy Ghost" (208
*AS*). Carr's moment of conversion substitutes the word "humility" for "sacrifice," but is otherwise virtually the same:
"Like all the blind materialists, the grabbers, the hogs and
donkeys of a society which he had despised and rejected, he
had despised in her [his wife] just that which made her
better than he—her humility, her faith. . . . With what gratitude for her love and sympathy, for all God's goodness and
the power of His Spirit, he joined with her in the crowning
verse" (29 *AS*).

Another parallel to Aissa's sacrifice is that of Ishe, a
woman who gives her son, Numi, to the goddess Oke. Ishe
is like Aissa in her excessive behavior: "when she quarrelled,
as happened every day, she showed such anger and ill will
that many people called her a witch" (34 *AS*). In a scene
parallel to the one in which Aissa sacrifices Abba, Ishe sacrifices Numi. Numi has been kidnapped by the ju-ju priestess,
and later Ishe is kidnapped herself while she is trying to
reach the district officer Bradgate. During a feast, filled with
drink, and song, Ishe is partly tricked, partly prevailed on to
utter the required phrase "I give Numi" (123 *AS*).

This scene, as well, is given quite externally; the action
is described minutely and there is no mention of motivation
at all:

Owule brought beer and she drank it thirstily like water.
The sweat was pouring from her. Her legs failed and she
tumbled down. The drummers came round her and beat
over her body, which writhed and jerked to the music. She
jumped up and ran about screaming: "Pity us—Oke, forgive

—send rain before we die"; then ran against the wall and cut her head open but did not faint.

They gave her more beer, and Owule said: "Brave Ishe, you save us, you help us, you give all—you give Numi."

The woman sighed: "I give all—I give Numi" (123 *AS*).

When the actual sacrifice comes, however, Ishe begins to struggle and scream, though her technical agreement to the sacrifice is unviolated since an assistant priest presses the veins in her neck so that she nearly faints and is certainly unable to speak.

The technique of showing actions as apart from motivation also shows the contrast. Ishe's action is in fact separate from her inner nature; it is an act without any meaning for her except tragedy. Aissa's sacrifice is in fact a direct expression of her inner nature, her devotion and faith, and is thus a product of what is best in her.

Ishe, in this sense, throws light on Aissa's nature precisely because she is an Aissa *manquée,* a woman without the necessary strength to go quite far enough in the direction her nature points out to her. That the direction is objectively a wrong one, makes no difference in the context of this book. Ishe stops before Aissa does, without, it might be added, gaining anything. Like Aissa she dies; like Aissa her son is sacrificed. The parallel between the two women exists primarily on the level of action; subjectively a wide gap separates them. Both the difference and the similarity are emphasized by the narrative voice which describes their actions externally, separate from inner meaning.

Of course, their common behavior has a good deal to do with their common background—both are brought up in a culture where education does not permit a great many choices and does not permit a full control over the environment. On the other hand, both have been brought up to regard sacrifice as a religious good, to consider child sacrifice as an act which affects the mother more than it does the child, and to believe that such a sacrifice is actually effective.

At the same time they are both the same kind of women, excessive in their actions, not quite committed to their surroundings and therefore, to a certain extent, freer than their neighbors. They are also more vulnerable, excessively attached to their children, and also excessively ready to work out in effective action their inner states.

In terms of the richness of their subjective life, on the other hand, a life to be evaluated and described only by reference to internal states rather than to action, Aissa wins hands down. Her giving of Abba is truly wholehearted, and comes after a thorough struggle within herself. The struggle, which in honesty to her character is shown as completely nonintellectual, is objectified in the scene where she talks with Jesus and desperately tries to cancel her commitment to Christianity. At first she talks of it as a finished business arrangement: "I do all ting for Jesus. Jesus say, 'You good girl, Aissa. You love me proper.' He give me Gajere, he give me Abba. I go home now. All done finish" (200 *AS*). Later she tries to fool Jesus by pretending that she loves herself more than Abba and Gajere and that by cutting herself she is making a major sacrifice: "I no lak Gajere at all. I you woman, Jesus. I give you all. I give you ma nose, I give you ma mouf. I no good for no man no mo" (202 *AS*). Still, later she tries to fool Jesus by throwing a rock into the river and pretending it is Abba. But throughout the course of this argument she is too much for herself. And that is the point. She will not allow herself to fool herself. She insists on the ultimate acting out of her devotion, perverted as that devotion is seen to be at the same time, and she goes far beyond the point at which Ishe has long since stopped. Her reward is not on the level of action, just as the value of her act is not on the level of action. She has lost her son and she dies, but she dies in joy, reaching for Abba: "Aissa held out her arms to him and shouted, 'Oh, you rascal.' She could not help laughing at him. She was helpless with laughter" (212 *AS*).[11]

The point of all this may well be not much more than that Christianity is more demanding than ju-ju, that it demands more of a sacrifice and especially a more wholehearted sacrifice, so that while a simple technical agreement to the sacrifice is enough to satisfy the ju-ju goddess, only a fully accepting agreement is adequate to satisfy Jesus. However, there seems to be also an evaluation of character here, one made over and over again by Cary's works: the character who follows his own direction furthest is also the one who is worthiest.

If the actions of Aissa and Ishe are seen as quite apart from their motivation, then another group is seen as if without any inner content at all. These are the soldiers, who play similar unthinking roles in several Cary books. Zeggi, for instance, the chief of police who had been a soldier for various sides—the shift of sides is typical in pointing up the lack of allegiance to political principle in Cary's soldiers—seems to be a man empty inside, without thought or feeling. He delivers messages to Bradgate as if their content made no difference at all. He sets out to heal Aissa at one time and to kill her at another as if there were no difference in the two. He even walks about as if he didn't realize what his own physical circumstances are. Although his body is old and ruined, "He swaggered about Yanrin, an old military fez cocked over one eye, with the lively gait and cheerful self-satisfaction of a corporal lady killer" (101 *AS*). In fact, Zeggi's only positive characteristic seems to be his devotion to orders: "He had grasped the notions of duty and obedience, of routine, and even the idea of them. . . . It was his religion, his touchstone, his glory" (102 *AS*).

A similar character is Dan Angass, the soldier assigned to help Ali, who is the young son of the Waziri and whose ethics come from the football field of his school. When Dan Angass, Ali, and a soldier named Suli are sent all by themselves to halt a riot and to do it without shooting, Angass is fully aware of the danger. Nevertheless he goes about the job, following the orders given by Ali, in a methodical way, all the while protesting that they will be killed. Ali is another character whose external actions are emphasized. He is not quite aware of the danger of the situation, and also not quite aware of his own motivation. Unlike Aissa, however, he is "perfectly cool" in his actions. Like other Cary heroes, especially soldier heroes, he escapes danger, and sometimes even awareness of danger, by being "closely preoccupied with his management of the enterprise . . ." (170 *AS*).

It is somewhat in the same way that in *Castle Corner* Cock Jarvis invades Laka and escapes the dangers of that march. In contrast, Jim Latter diverts Nina's attention from the danger of a stormy sail by emphasizing the action, but the fact is that he is himself quite terrified and uses the device only to make Nina settle down.

The third voice in the narration carries the burden of knowledge and gives the sense not only that the world exists but also that it can be known and that people can be understood. In fact it is this voice which really matches the traditional voice of the omniscient narrator because it suggests the knowability of events.

On the one hand this narrator has the kind of knowledge which comes from superior and lengthy research. Thus he can give the history, background and general characteristics of the various characters. He knows, for instance, that Ojo's "passions were not mixed with calculation" (16 *AS*), that Musa is "proud of his position as headman" (36 *AS*), that Jacob "had a great respect for himself" (78–9 *AS*). He speaks with authority in these cases, but most of the evaluations of this sort are not of deep insight and do not give away many secrets. In fact, it would be quite easy—if Cary wanted not to grant such authority to his narrator—to avoid this kind of statement and provide the same information in other ways. However, there is a tone of omniscience given by this narrator which goes deeper, and this tone results from a typical Cary turn of phrase which lasts throughout many books. By using such phrases as: "In this she was right . . ." (48 *AS*), "What had happened was this . . ." (197 *AS*), and "But in fact . . ." (161 *AS*), the works repeatedly suggest that there is a level of ascertainable and unquestioned truth.

Often these phrases suggest that the official version of the facts is wrong and that the true facts are now to be given by the narrator. The official report on the riots at Kolu, for instance, praises the emir and his councillors for their moderation. The truth is, however, that they were not moderate at all. The narrator says, "But in fact they were taken by surprise in the first place, and afterwards being summoned in council they could not decide on a common policy" (161 *AS*).

This same voice also refuses to speak with authority on occasion, as when Carr is ignored in his attempt to stop the natives from leaving for Kolu: *"probably* no one noticed him" (22 *AS*; my italics). Even this removal of authority, however, suggests a level on which definite knowledge exists.

Aside from these various tones with which the narrator speaks—a matter which is connected to the moral effect the book produces—there is the other dimension of the shift in point of view, a matter which is more closely connected with the formal requirement of the book. The basic formal design of this book, like that of the other early works, is based on the invasion of one group by another. This device shows the true relationship between the various forces operating in the larger social scene and on individual human beings. Cary's effect requires that the reader understand the situation and accept it. Thus he describes each force from the inside, from within its own point of view, justifying it by showing it within its own terms. The technique leads to an objective acceptance by the reader of widely varying sociological, and later, personal, patterns. As a result, the conflicts which follow seem inevitable; the difference between the sides is so wide. But in another sense the conflicts seem also ironically silly; the disparity is so wide that people most of the time are not fighting the battle they think they are involved in. Furthermore, they often share basic human patterns which show them —again ironically—to be much more similar, under all the differences, than anyone caught in the conflict is able to suppose.

The opening of *Aissa Saved* prepares for the invasion which is to come. An examination of what might well be considered the first section of the novel, chapters 1–14 (13– 66 *AS*), will indicate the nature of the procedure. The first four chapters deal with the Christians, both the Carrs and the native converts. The section fulfills multiple requirements, three of which call for special discussion. First, the plot of the book requires an invasion, and so the central question in this section is whether the Christians will go or not, and the section ends with all the various parts of the group (Mr. Carr, rationalist; Mrs. Carr, emotionalist; Ojo, the convert of great faith; Aissa, either a trollop or of excessively affectionate nature) united in hymn singing as they sail towards Kolu.

Second, the theme requires that the nature of this force in Africa be explained, and so the section shows the difficulty the Carrs feel they have in operating without the full blessing of the official British administration; it also shows that their converts are mostly those who are misfits in their own society (and thus appear to others, for instance the Kolua, as rejected scum); and it shows the actual difficulty of transmitting Christianity to this foreign, illiterate culture.

Third, the thesis requires a conflict between the simple faith of Mrs. Carr and the rational attitudes of Mr. Carr, and so the question of whether to go or not is bound up with this opposition.[12]

All three of these points are central to the book and all are developed carefully. The book as a whole thus traces the conflict between the forces of this society in transition. Aissa's fate develops as it does because she is a misfit in both the Christian society (which she misunderstands as requiring literal sacrifice) and her own society (where she fits neither personally nor ideologically), because the British administration, in the person of Bradgate, has not fully taken responsibility for running the country, and because Aissa submits to her emotional, illogical, disordered need for sacrifice. It is paradoxical that her failure lies so close to her triumph, which has as its source her ultimate willingness to follow herself, her accession to her own nature, even to the sacrifice of her own life, her lover, and her child.

With all these matters clearly established, with the reader firmly understanding that the desires and needs of the Christian group arise out of understandable, human patterns

working within a specific situation, and with the potential invasion set, this section has now done its part. The angle of
vision of the book therefore shifts, and the next section opens
quite as if nothing had preceded it, in the pagan town of
Kolu, the target of the Christians. The people of Kolu are
now presented in reaction to their overriding problem, that
of the drought. They are shown as resourceful by the authoritative narrator: "The Kolua are an intelligent, brave people.
They know that every effect has a cause, and they are not
prepared to call any cause hopeless of improvement" (30
*AS*). In general the Kolua are also shown as living a normal
life. Within their group their way is standard. Since, however,
it is Cary's way to present conflict as often as possible, because
conflict is everywhere as the necessary consequence of freedom, this section shows differences too. For instance, there is
a wide disparity between the ordinary people who only discuss matters, the priests who take the radical action (sanc-
tioned by tradition though it is, of kidnapping a boy for a
sacrifice to the goddess Oke), and the village headman, Musa,
who tries to stop the kidnapping because of the opposition
which he knows will come from the white administration.
Ironically, thus, the leaders of the pagans are shown to have
their difficulties with the secular order just as the Carrs have
their problems with Bradgate.

It is only after this second part has brought the reader
firmly within the point of view of the pagan natives, thus
justifying their way of life, that the Christian group arrives,
seen from the point of view of the Kolua people.

Even though this invasion leads to general misunderstanding and violence, there is a level of narration which
makes it obvious that there are fundamental human patterns
which are the same for all. The story of Jesus, for instance,
is one of universal human significance, and its telling is effective. "They [the pagans] had heard every word and followed the story with the closest interest. It interested them
so much that they wanted to hear it again, in order to find
out what it meant" (43 *AS*). Aissa's joy in finding her man,

Gajere, who had stayed in Kolu, is picked up by the crowd and turns into a large-scale dance.

In general, however, there is misunderstanding. For instance, Brimah, a native pagan who has spent some time at the mission and who can therefore help fellow Kolua understand the Christians, explains the working of the Trinity. The Spirit, he carefully explains is sometimes "like fire, and sometimes like a white goat" (40 *AS*). It is also

> God's Waziri. He does the dirty work, runs messages, chases after you when you don't do what you're told. I know because he caught me one day at Shibi when I was drunk in a beer-house there. He jumped up my nose before I knew where I was. He was like a hot wind, and when he got inside me, he took me by the throat so that I nearly choked . . . (40–41 *AS*).

He again helps out by summarizing the sermon in which Ojo tells the people that if they pray to Jesus, Jesus will ask "God to forgive [them] and send [them] the rain" (42 *AS*). Brimah explains: "Why, he says that all you pagan people are damn bad people and that's why God spoils your crops and stops the rain. . . . And unless you turn Christian and give God a good sacrifice like Jesus, you'll be starved out" (43 *AS*).

Brimah's religious vision here is not far from what Aissa's develops into later. Like Brimah fighting with the Holy Ghost, she argues with God inside of her. Like Brimah, she takes for granted the necessity of giving God a sacrifice. Like Brimah, too, she makes the confusion of goat and Ghost, with the implicit suggestion that the goat refers also to the sacrificial scapegoat, which Aissa eventually becomes.

After the initial appearance of the Christians, the point of view switches rapidly among the Carrs, the native crowds who are watching, Aissa, Musa, the crowd surrounding Aissa, and others. The effect is one of lack of direction, as the riot itself is essentially undirected,[13] and of violence.

The use of the angle of vision in the opening section of *Aissa Saved* then is carefully worked out, to explain the

forces within their own context, and to show the wide difference between the various views as well as the similarities
lying beneath the human pattern of behavior. The section
is ended, without really being concluded, by the simple device
of following a little girl, Tanawe, a cousin of the kidnapped
boy, on her trip to Bradgate in order to get help.[14]

This next section continues in the same pattern and
explains the third large group in Kolu, that of the administration, Bradgate and his entire milieu. It might be noted here
that seen in his own situation Bradgate is as much justified
as the others are. Considering his total situation—for instance,
the difficulties he has with the Emir, whose main characteristic
is a resigned melancholy, and with the servants around him,
whom he doesn't trust but whom he has to depend on nevertheless—he is seen not at all as a bad man to be blamed but
rather as a man doing the normal expected job.

It is only after this that the story resumes with the imprisonment of Aissa, her later escape, the repeated invasion
of Kolu, the final riot, and then concludes with Aissa's apoth-
eosis.

## II

The shifting of the angle of vision which has such clear
simple purpose in *Aissa Saved* is used in the later books as well,
though with each book Cary developed the technique further.
A major development came in *Mister Johnson* and another in
the trilogies. As in *Aissa Saved*, too, the narration of the other
works maintains a variety of tones.

In *An American Visitor*, for instance, it is the objective
voice, which describes only what the eyes can see and the
ears can hear, which narrates the first attack of the Birri
natives on the whites:

> Marie was turning to run back to the fort when she saw, to
> her astonishment and horror, Bewsher set out at full speed
> towards the Birri, holding out his arms like a man trying to
> turn a flock of sheep, and shouting at the top of his voice
> expostulations in the strongest language. Beside him Obai
> galloped uttering a war-yell and poising his spear. . . .

[Gore] saw Bewsher about ten yards away beating somebody with the shaft of a broken spear, and he saw Marie, to his great surprise, rushing towards Bewsher. . . .

But all this was like a snapshot taken by the light of the burning roof between his discovery that he was not dead yet and that the Birri did not appear inclined to kill him, and the terrific blow which now fell on the top of his head and seemed to drive him into the ground (135–36 *Am V*).[15]

There is also the voice in *An American Visitor* which suggests the dimension of the unquestionably knowable. This is the voice which knows, for instance, that it is not true that the remains shipped back to Marie as Bewsher's belonged to a pagan: "This was a slander" (233 *Am V*).

On the whole, though, *An American Visitor* limits its authoritative statements by locating the narrator in one of the characters of the story. The description of the action during the confrontation of Bewsher and the pagans just cited, for instance, comes from the point of view of Marie Hasluck, the visitor from America, and of Gore, assistant to the resident. In addition, there seems also to be an attempt in this book to make Cottee a major narrating center and to channel the bulk of the information through him. There seems no special reason for doing this, no more reason at any rate than there was in *Aissa Saved* to place the narrating center in a character in the story. On the other hand, Cary obviously has a continuing interest in providing information through his characters and in avoiding, much of the time, speaking in the narrator's voice. This tendency becomes more emphatic from *The African Witch* on.

Why Cottee, Marie and Gore should have been especially chosen is not quite clear, and why there should be this special attempt to avoid the authority of the narrator is also not clear. Nevertheless it is there, though far from being total throughout the book. For instance, as in *Aissa*, Cary switches frequently to the natives so that their motivations will become clear from within their own situation. Thus Uli's difficulty in making love to his wife face to face is shown from within the native angle of vision (57–59 *Am V*). The suggestions which accompany this incident become a leading motif throughout the book—as does Johnson's attempt to Europeanize his wife—because it shows what happens when a native African comes under the influence of foreign culture. Free enough to accept a new, perhaps even a better, way of showing affection, Uli affronts a fundamental part of the conservative culture he is still connected to. As a result, this strong, assured warrior becomes an example of the disorderly confusion which follows the Europeanization of Africa. Manners deteriorate, people are confused. Uli himself becomes a Christian temporarily, a surly one with a mistress whom he beats because of his own frustration. Though he is a member of the Europeanized community he has no real commitment to it. In fact he soon escapes and rejoins his own people amongst whom he seems again to find his proper place. In spite of what he feels, however, he does not regain the past, because the total situation has changed. He takes part in his people's attack on Bewsher in the name of Birri nationalism, an act which in turn brings the mining concession in and will no doubt spread the effects of civilization more widely and rapidly. Just how destructive these effects are on the existing culture can be seen in the example of Henry, who has been in close contact with the Europeans and who advises at least one native to marry incestuously. "In the great world outside Birri men are not afraid to take what they want," he says (163 *Am V*), misapplying but not really totally misunderstanding European culture.

The Gore point of view in a sense is opposed to the Cottee point of view, because Gore and Cottee are fundamentally different personalities, who relate to life differently. The difference is central to this book and to Cary in general. Gore is a man of traditional sensibilities and values; Cottee is rather like a European Henry, a revolutionary who cares very little for any artificial system of values or ethics.[16] The difference between them can be seen as Cottee peeps at Bewsher and Marie when they are just beginning their affair. "But Gore did not see any excuse either for humour or peeping" (86 *Am V*), and he interrupts the peeping by calling loudly to the two. In a very similar way, Gore is shocked by the natives who make themselves spectators at an argument between himself and Bewsher (43 *Am V*). Again, he cuts Cottee when Cottee tries to discuss Marie personally (154 *Am V*). He is a compromiser without firm intellectual commitments but with lots of traditional principles. He is at his job largely because it is traditional for his family to serve the country rather than because he has any specific proposals to carry out. One of the mining prospectors tells him, "I quite realize that you've got to amuse yourself with something, and this Birri game is better than golf or spillikins," and he agrees: "Jukes had hit the nail" (48 *Am V*). Cottee describes Gore's family as one of traditional servants of the state: "parsons, soldiers, doctors, civil servants, magistrates, none of them rich; their whole inheritance a few old swords, bibles, medals and stories" (235 *Am V*). Still, he is devoted to doing his job as effectively as he can. He heroically sticks to principle when he refuses to send for the soldiers, against the emotional desires of nearly everyone at the station. He is in fact a superior civil servant, doing his best under often difficult circumstances, against the opposition of his superiors, his friends, and his countrymen, with nothing but traditional, unthoughtout principles to guide him. In fact he is a stock figure, the somewhat bumbling Englishman whose decency comes to him by a kind of inheritance and informal education. He is an embodiment of the tradition which is bound to be broken by history, just as the traditional civilization of the Birri is bound to be broken by the "progress" articulated by Henry. Not only is Gore the good kind of British civil servant; he is also an embodiment of the principles of the Foreign Service which administers its African possessions without any plan, but with decent principles worked out *ad hoc*.[17] In this he is specifically opposed to Bewsher, the man who always fights his own administration, because he is obsessed by a positive vision which is, in fact, to produce an artificial civilization for the Birri. As Cottee puts it, "And so you put them [the Birri] in a sort of human zoo—Mappin terraces for interesting pagan specimens" (88 *Am V*). Part of Bewsher's program is to keep all exploiters and missionaries out of the area while he prepares them for complex modern civilization step by step. He will give them a new nationalism based on their tribal unity, and he will even manufacture for them a new religion based on their old one; for example, it is suggested that he might turn "the thunder god Ogun into the god or more strictly the Saint of Electricity and Vital Energy" (132 *Am V*), thus grafting beliefs in modern science, as well as ethics, on the traditional Birri religion.[18] Thus, intellectually, Bewsher offers an alternative to the nondirected system of administration of the Foreign Service. Emotionally, too, he offers opposition to Gore. Rather than accepting the status quo and helping to sustain it, like Gore, Bewsher is one of the men of imagination, who, like Aissa, translate their feelings and visions into reality. Like Aissa, too, he is a man of excessive action, a man with a strong sense of life, and his first appearance—a dangerous leap from a dugout into a ship—is typical of his ability to arouse excitement by his daring and courage.

Cottee is a very different sort of man. He is from the same sort of family as Gore, but he has detached himself from their traditions (235 *Am V*). Essentially he is an intellectual who has taken the step of action.[19] Interestingly enough, Cottee's intellectual views coincide with Cary's throughout the book. He attacks the system which refuses to give to the African natives the physical advantages of civilization which they themselves are anxious to have.[20] At the same time he argues against the system which has denied to the natives widespread education (97 *Am V*). Though he does not express any awareness of Cary's second thoughts—the difficulties which follow education and civilization—his views are nevertheless Cary's.

Cottee also voices Cary's views when he explains that the general abstractions which underlie the specific systems of civilization are always the same, though the specific forms vary with history. He says explicitly, "What Marie calls Beudy, truth and goodness are always the same. But religions and

nations can be as different as cathedrals and pigsties. . . ."
He adds that, "we all depend on rather elaborate constructions of tradition and poetry and art and religion for our possibilities of feeling—the quality of our feelings about things,
the quality of our lives . . ." (152 *Am V*).

It is also Cottee who predicts exactly what Marie will do
when he says, at first in general,

> That when a civilization or an old palace gets a bit out of
> repair or knocked about in an earthquake the people who
> live in it, just because they've been so comfortable and grand,
> have forgotten all about practical bricklaying; and the in-
> spired odd job-man who rushes in to clean up the mess, just
> because he *is* a practical enthusiast, doesn't give a damn for
> architecture or any of those frills. Practical enthusiasts never
> do. They're too energetic and original and self-reliant. They
> go by common sense—that's to say they consult the inner
> light about the drains (152 *Am V*).

A moment later he specifically evaluates Marie as one of these
inner light mystics,

> . . . with the strongest kind of religious instincts and no
> theology [from whom] you can expect the worst. Imagine the
> demons and wishfulfilment djinns that arise from their sub-
> conscious, shouting "Do what you will and all will be well.
> Follow your lusts and they will make you whole"—all the
> modern gospel. The complete nature god. The whole Shel-
> leyan formula. Down with all creeds. Bring in the golden
> age. Free love and no more clothes (153 *Am V*).

This basically does describe Marie's notions, and does
point to the failure by which she gets Monkey Bewsher killed
when she refuses to give him his revolver because she has just
been converted to the religion of love. Her failure, of course,
is not one of belief. It is rather precisely what Cottee has here
described. She is consulting the inner light about the drains.
That is, she is trying to deal with reality without being aware
of what reality is like, and is applying raw principles. She has
come up against this problem a number of times and in one
conversation, alluded to at the time she does not bring the

gun, Bewsher has had to correct her ignorance of the actual conditions of life: "He had looked like that when she had first produced her theory that the Birri civilization was the natural pattern of society" (227 *Am V*). Bewsher never makes the mistake of thinking that things happen by abstract principles, real as such principles may be. Thus, he tells Marie, the Birri civilization is far from being run by cooperation, or by natural principle; rather "it's a whole man's job seeing that people learn the rules and keep them and pass them on . . ." (90 *Am V*).[21]

In his view of history Cottee agrees with Cary, too. For instance, he says about the Birri,

> . . . even if civilization meant for the Birri a meaner shallower kind of life, how could any man hope to fight against it when it came with the whole drive of the world behind it, bringing every kind of gaudy toy and easy satisfaction (234 *Am V*).

He sees what later becomes the basis of one important portion of Cary's historical works, that while individual forms change with history, the root principles, like beauty, art, devotion, for instance, are "as indestructible and as fertile as life itself" (235 *Am V*).[22] At the same time he mentions also Cary's view that individuals, in spite of all this, live in their own time, "made of sentiments and attachments and associations which by their very nature could not be transferred. The greater a period, the stronger the allegiance and interdependence of its human parts . . ." (235 *Am V*).[23] In spite of this coincidence of views between Cottee and Cary, Cottee is far from being a sympathetic character. Besides not being a gentleman, being what is even worse, a black sheep of a gentlemanly family, Cottee lacks the force of personality to match his intellectual insights. Both Marie and Gore make this same point: Marie says, "Cottee was clever, but he was outside things. He didn't really feel them" (95 *Am V*).[24] Gore echoes Marie, and though he speaks specifically only of religion, the judgment obviously is also a general one:

He was always bored with Cottee on the subject of religion; not because Cottee did not know a great deal more about it than himself but because he was not religious. He had no experience of religion and so he did not really know anything about it and his words though they might be true had no importance or interest (151 *Am V*).[25]

These views, since they come from two characters rather than from any outside source, might in themselves be less than fully convincing. But actually, nothing in the book contradicts their general view. Cottee is very much the outsider. He loses the girl, his major desire is for money, and he seems shallow in contrast with Bewsher's and Marie's more complete dedication to life itself. Indeed, Cottee is so much out of things in the book that he seems to be drawn much more fully in intellectual terms than is necessary for his role in the story. Any kind of character, without any special historical views, that is, could assume the role of the entrepreneur attempting to open Africa to trade.

Rather than for the plot, then, Cottee is needed for his ideas, so that they may serve as a standard in contrast to Marie and Bewsher, just as Gore stands in contrast to Marie and Bewsher by presenting normal standards of personal dedication. In this sense both men serve as devices, foils to throw light on the situation of Bewsher and Marie.

While it is clear that Cottee is less acceptable as a character than as a thinker, it is not so clear why Cottee is undercut so consistently, why he is presented with such thorough irony. Part of the answer may well be Cary's reluctance to portray the intellectual in completely positive terms. Cottee may also be the victim of Cary's general tone of condescension for junior officers, a condescension directed also towards Gore here, as well as towards Rudbeck in *Mister Johnson* and Fisk in *The African Witch*.[26]

What may be of greater importance in terms of Cary's developing style is that we find him attempting here to work out a form in which he introduces ideas into a book through a character who represents his own views fairly closely. Cary has often mentioned his problems with ideas in books. First he had the problem of developing the proper ones; then he had the problem of keeping them within proper bounds; indeed he sometimes sounds as if a major problem was how to excise the ideas from his works.[27] Here, obviously, Cary was not only trying to dramatize his ideas by presenting them in his characters, but he was trying also to apologize for them, as it were, by ironically undercutting the character who expresses them. Thus, a character who is *not* heroic seems to have more right to ideas than one who is, perhaps because it seems fairer. In a sense it may also be simpler, since such a minor character could not be required to be as fully developed, to act out his ideas as fully as major characters like, say, Marie and Bewsher.

It is through Cottee that Cary leaves the final impression of the story. It is he who sees and variously evaluates Marie and, through her, Bewsher. He first sees her as existing on another level of being than the ordinary:

> It [her voice] transported him once more into another state of being, where men and women were born to heroic destinies, and life was the magnificent stage of their glories and their suffering; and it seemed to him, moreover, that the men and women who lived in this other romantic world, call them sentimentalists if you like, were the only ones who knew how to live at all. The rest were the cowards, like himself, who were afraid to love, who were afraid of being laughed at; who mutilated and tamed within themselves every wild creature of the spirit in order to be in safe and comfortable possession of their own farmyard and on good terms with the neighbors (238 *Am V*).

A moment later he quickly gets another view:

> Cottee could now look at her. She had slipped her wrist out of his arm. He half turned towards her, gazed sharply and curiously at the small white face, the big sensitive lips made relatively bigger by the thinness of the cheeks. But no, the fancy dissolved like a transformation scene. This ugly little woman a tragic queen, Monkey Bewsher a hero, it was absurd (238 *Am V*).[28]

Only Cottee, of the characters in the book, could have had this double reaction. Gore is too gentlemanly to have either view, and also too closely connected with Marie. Also, Cottee is probably the only one to have the width—which is not at all the same as the depth—to have the double view. In the first of these two views, he sees her subjectively, from the inside, as a woman who has gone all the way with her beliefs. She has been first an anarchist, whose only notion was to find a natural way of life and substitute that for civilization. Later she has changed this view in a scene which is supported by a memorable shift of images. Her early view of idealized Greece gives way to an image of Greek civilization as "Galleys full of agonized rowers bleeding under the whip—chained to battered leaking ships—kept from sinking altogether only by the endless patching and plugging of the anxious carpenters creeping about with their tools in the stinking bilges" (193–94 *Am V*). Finally she becomes converted to the view that love is an active force, which can be depended on in a crisis over guns. In each transformation she was surely guilty of the excessive emotionalism, that same lack of real acceptance of the world, which characterized Aissa. In each one, on the other hand, she has given herself fully, and has taken chances beyond the normal, also like Aissa.

Cottee's double view, thus, corresponds to her double quality. Seen visually, objectively, for her action alone, she is absurd. Seen inwardly, for the wealth of her spirit, her mythical human quality, she is a heroine. And in seeing her in this double way, Cottee the narrator also sees in two of the three ways typical of the Cary narration.

*The African Witch* has the look of a novel in which the author narrates the story in his own voice and keeps firm control over all material. This comes partly from the seemingly leisurely narration at the opening, where a character is no sooner mentioned than he is further described. For instance, Rackham appears two paragraphs after he is mentioned by Mrs. Pratt: "Oh! where is Captain Rackham? He's the only man who really knows how to deal with such people" (15 *Af W*). And the narration shows him in the traditional way, externally, by giving a physical description first and then by describing his relationship to Judy Coote.

Similarly, no sooner is the resident, Burwash, described by Mrs. Pratt as the kind of politician who tends to evade issues, than he is shown doing exactly that.

An additional sense of narrative control is given by the tendency in this book, as in other Cary works, to begin a section with a general summarizing statement and then to show the details. Thus the effect is of preparing the reader for information and then giving it to him, so that he comes to trust the narration. The opening sentence, for instance, states that "An awkward incident took place at Rimi races" (15 *Af W*), while the section continues with a description of that incident and thus fills in the outlines of the rough sketch, as it were. Again, a description of the facts behind the riot in town is prefaced with the words, "What had happened in Rimi was that . . ." (49 *Af W*). Authority is further established by such phrases as, "It was quite true that . . ." (26 *Af W*), "This was a lie" (82 *Af W*), and "But this was not true" (16 *Af W*), which appear frequently.

In fact, however, while the narration has the tone of certifiable omniscience, it has little of the content, and a closer examination of the narration shows a curious division between establishing authority and refusing to be authoritative.

The authority established is more than offset by what is either inability or unwillingness to accept responsibility for knowledge. Sometimes the narrator refuses to speak in his own voice and makes a point of having a character in the book assume responsibility for an evaluation or statement. The analysis of Burwash's ability to rid himself of people he doesn't want to talk to without causing ill will, thus is given to Rackham: "Rackham's theory was that his success in the art of shunting depended entirely on that long straightening action which withdrew his face out of immediate intimacy" (46 *Af W*). In the same way, it is Rackham, not the narrator, who describes Mrs. Vowls as a crank, and it is he who characterizes one of her motions as "her hostess gesture" (70, 71 *Af W*). It is quite in tune with Rackham as a character that he should be involved in both of these cases. The first shows his tendency to put things in physical terms; Judy, on the contrary, explains Burwash's ability not to offend the people he abruptly dismisses in terms very different from Rackham's: "People like the Resident because he's friendly" (46 *Af W*). There is also adequate reason for Rackham's involvement in the evaluation of Mrs. Vowls. She is the anarchist who represents one side of the difference between Judy and Dryas, which is also one side of his divided self as it is of Aladai's, and it is her name Rackham calls up when he finally has his insight into Dryas' nonrational personality: "Vowls. . . . What am I thinking of? . . . quite a different type. . . . All the same . . . Mrs. Vowls—there's a taste of her there" (268 *Af W*).[29] Granted that the remarks are suitable for Rackham, it is still true that his making them is a kind of intrusion which detracts from the narrator's authority, especially since Rackham is not even present at the scene with Mrs. Vowls. Similarly, the popularity of the missionary, Schlemm, is explained not by the narrator but by Rackham ("that Norfolk suit and beard have put him over"), by Rubin ("Nobody could help liking the old beak. He's a Christian"), and by Colour-Sergeant Root ("he was a real gentleman") (128 *Af W*).

At other times the narrator seems simply not to know, and the ascription of information to other characters is paralleled by a frequent tendency of the narration not to be sure of events, or of their meaning. For example, when Rackham jolts Fisk into the hold, he does it *"probably* by design" (207 *Af W*).[30] The events involving a fight between Coker's party and Aladai's are uncertain: "What happened in Rimi the rest of that morning is not exactly known" (218 *Af W*).

Perhaps the most significant moments of ignorance come when the narrator limits his knowledge carefully to a simple level, and refuses to go further. For instance when Rackham is discussing his objections to native Africans who are Europeanized, the narrator knows that the reason he gives is not the real one. Still, having gone so far as to announce what is not true, he will not go further to tell what is true. Agreeing with something Dryas has said, Rackham says the "trousered apes" are bad copies. "But Rackham did not really believe that the copies were all bad. His objection was deeper. He did not examine it" (45 *Af W*). Again, it is in character for Rackham not to examine his beliefs. First, he is the typical Englishman in Africa who does not really know what he is doing there or what his attitudes towards Africans ought to be. More important, only one side of him is drawn to Judy's intelligent self-awareness; more basically he is an external, physical, nonintrospective man, as is shown in part by his attraction to the physical Dryas. Furthermore, his unarticulated and unaware jealousy of natives is the rest of his problem, and the root of his blow-up with Aladai. Though the lack of insight is in character, however, it is still to be noted that the narration makes a point of remaining ignorant.

Exactly the same kind of half knowledge is given in the case of Coker. In explanation of his inability to give the full background of one of Coker's decisions, the narrator says that "Coker's motives were always obscure because though he had a reason for everything he did, and seemed to believe it himself, it was seldom the true one" (49 *Af W*). Later Coker's motives are speculated about in such a way as to remove responsibility from the narrator:

> It seemed odd to suggest that Coker's real motive in murdering several white people was to provoke reprisals, and so bring the necessary suffering upon Africa. This theory could not be proved, of course, because Coker's motives were unknown to himself; but it was suggested by a man who knew something about morbid psychology and primitive religion—which are nearly the same thing (209 *Af W*).

This passage contains two interesting clues about the technique of Cary at this stage. One is that he will introduce a character who appears nowhere else in the novel, not even by name, as an authority to suggest, not to state, be it noted, an insight into a character. This refusal becomes even more noteworthy in light of the narrator's perfect willingness at the same time to accept responsibility for the general statement that morbid psychology and primitive religion are nearly the same thing.

The other clue is that the narrator is careful to explain that the reason Coker's motivation could not be proved is that it was unknown to himself. The implication is that if Coker were the sort of man to know himself, the narrator would feel free to describe him more deeply. Apparently, then, a narrator may enter the consciousness of his characters to explain them only insofar as they are aware of themselves. Coker's actions, because they are external, can be shown, but his internal confusion can only be indicated. The same is true of Rackham. Clear-cut insight into him stops where his self awareness stops. On the other hand, we can clearly see the acted out division in Aladai when he is drawn between ju-ju emotion and rationality, because he is aware of this division within himself. Again, Judy, because she has more insight into herself, can be seen much more clearly and deeply than Dryas.

This fairly consistent technique in *The African Witch* suggests strongly that there is no clear division between Cary's first person narration in the trilogies and the "omniscient" narration in the earlier works. Here he is telling the story in the third person but holding the narration to the limits of his characters' awareness, and this is precisely one of the major effects of first person narration. In the trilogies, on the other hand, a voice beyond the first person narrator's obviously makes itself felt with something of the effect of omniscience when the individual novels are read together as trilogy.[31]

The strange division between full knowledge and ignorance does not seem to interfere with the voice of the tourist guide narrator. On the contrary, *The African Witch* is perhaps fuller than any other Cary book of this kind of information. This narrator, for instance, tells that real women are extremely curious (24 *Af W*), that most women are conservative (36 *Af W*), that the African standard of beauty is baroque and not Greek (29 *Af W*), that no one really knows within a thousand years how old Rimi is (79 *Af W*), that the

Africans who desire white men's clothing are the most enterprising of their group (149 *Af W*), that in an autocratic
court the difficulties of moving from one ruler to the next
presents the insurmountable problem of how to buy trust
with treachery (176–77 *Af W*), and that Negroes sleep more
deeply than whites (257 *Af W*).

The most unexpected touch of this sort is the obvious
attempt to prove in the context of the book that extrasensory
perception does work, an attempt supported by Ibu's finding
of Elizabeth entirely by sensing her "calls" (272–75 *Af W*).[32]

Cary's insistently informative tone in this book is not
unusual for him. But though he tends to give information
about history and sociology throughout his work, he emphasizes this side of his interest in *The African Witch* beyond
the two earlier books. *Castle Corner* attempts to push even
further in the same sociological direction, and its failure apparently convinced Cary to backtrack with *Mister Johnson*.[33]

The voice of the narrator whose description is limited
to what he can see and hear also presents a significant development in *The African Witch*; it is largely, perhaps paradoxically, connected with the intellectual Judy, who serves
as an angle of vision throughout the book. It is she, for instance, who sees Aladai's heroic behavior during the riot which
she has helped start when she innocently brought Aladai into
town. Because she cannot understand the language, and because she cannot really comprehend what is happening in the
strange place where she thought herself a sightseer and has
found herself provoking a political riot, she grasps the scene
primarily as sight and sound. She grasps it, that is, as external
action and is unable at this stage to have any real understanding of its political, social, or even human significance.[34]
She performs roughly the same function again when she becomes a purely visual observer of Coker's religious meeting
(348 *Af W*).

The most significant occasion of the use of this objective
technique comes when Judy sees the old Emir. As the most
extreme example of the visual technique, the Emir is seen
not only as an actor without motivation, but as an actor who

is object rather than a human being. Actually the Emir does not play a significant part in the plot of the story. He is necessary to provide the element that must be removed before anyone succeeds him; at the same time he has to be rather powerless (so that the issue can remain primarily between Aladai and Salé) and old (so that the necessity of finding a successor is immediate). He is more a requirement of the sociological side of the book, then, than of the formal side. What is seen of him helps to describe the total situation within which Aladai works out his political and personal struggle. Perhaps because he is in himself such an insignificant figure Cary tried a daring experiment with him. More than with any other character in his work—and for the first time here—Cary shows in the emir a man from two entirely different viewpoints, one entirely internal, one entirely external.

The attempt deserves closer inspection. Judy first sees him as part of a confused "show" full of "mounted officials, courtiers, townsmen." The Emir is part of a tableau formed by his horse, "a huge black stallion . . . [which] reared at every pace." He himself is "a billowing mass of white, out of which a single bird-claw of a hand projected." A moment later he is part of another tableau, this time of bowing courtiers and of rich colors. He himself appears

> like a pillow balanced on its bottom edge and carrying on its other a smaller, rounder pillow. Between the two a little black crescent, three inches long and two wide, could be seen. This was his eyes and the bridge of his nose—all that was left uncovered of the royal face.

During the following meeting between the emir with his court and Burwash, the Emir is not once heard to speak, although the Vizier talks as if he has heard his instructions. When he leaves, he is again seen as a pillow which reels and falls until it appears again on the leaping horse as a "little white bundle firmly secured between the cantles of its huge saddle" (72–77 *Af W*).

In describing the emir in this nonhuman way, the scene points ironically to the emptiness of the position for which

Aladai and Salé are fighting.[35] But this is only a minor part of its effect. The scene is also fundamentally comic, especially in the context of Henri Bergson's insistence that comedy requires an absence of the human. "The attitudes, gestures, and movements of the human body are laughable in exact proportion as that body reminds us of a mere machine," Bergson says in a passage which might well serve as a formula for the description of the Emir here.[36] Also applicable with special relevance here is Bergson's further statement that, "We laugh every time a person gives us the impression of being a thing." [37] His best known and most concise definition of comedy, as *"Something mechanical encrusted on the living,"* [38] is even more to the point because of its suggestion that the comic requires a double element, the mechanical *and* the living. This duality is very much a part of the Emir's characterization; while seen here, and also later, only as mechanical, the emir is seen at other times as a human being fully justified in his own situation, and not more mechanical than many others.[39]

In his death scene he is also seen as object. After appearing as "a small white object" and after staggering around the town square, he is fed poison; "then he fell down, rolled over on his back, kicked up his little legs, and lay dead in that position, like a beetle" (228 *Af W*).

In Chapter 16, however, he is seen as quite alive and quite humanly understandable. Though he is very old, and no longer as capable as he once was, he certainly does not appear mechanical. He does have a very limited view, and he does think himself much more important than he is, it is true. Yet he is described explicitly—in this case in the voice of the knowing narrator himself—as a man of "purposeful activity of mind and body" (178 *Af W*). He is active and he still has a relationship with his old wife, Fanta, who remembers his days of youthful strength and heroism. Though he is much older, he is not seen here as significantly less alive or less human than, say, the emir of *Aissa Saved*.

That he is shown as mechanical at one time, and as alive at another may be due partly to metaphorical exaggeration. Though alive as a person, he has no more political force, no more influence on events, than a pillow. But there is also something else here, something which is typical of Cary in general. It is the two-sided simultaneous view: From the point of view of the purely visual narrator, and seen only on the level of action, the Emir is comic—"the mechanical encrusted on the living." However, seen from the point of view of the all-knowing narrator (seen, that is, from the inside), he is a meaningful human being. The tense confusion which results from looking at him from both sides simultaneously is a typical Cary effect.

The philosophical implication supported by the two narrating voices is that man has a double nature—human being or object, hero or fool, tragic or comic—which depends on the angle of vision, on whether the view is from the outside or the inside. Thus Cottee blinks and like an optical illusion his view of Marie Hasluck changes. Thus, too, Aissa is a silly girl, a misunderstanding rice-Christian, murderess of her child, but at the same time a noble human being of true religious faith.

The emir seems almost to be described in this way in order to make the abstract point, and as a character who is seen as both object and subject he is an example of an often repeated type. This type is the sinner whose life is explained in his book. Gulley, Tabitha, Sara, Wilcher, Nina, Charley, Aissa, Johnson, all the important Cary heroes are justified sinners—not justified in a sense which removes their guilt objectively, but justified in the sense that seen from within their own context their behavior is natural; they are seen, that is, as human, not mechanical but alive: in the words of Wylie Sypher, "an assertion of the flesh and its vitality . . . a Carrying Away of Death, a triumph over mortality by some absurd faith in rebirth, restoration, and salvation. . . ." [40]

But just as it is proper to say that Cary typically justifies the sinner, so would it also be right to say that he does not permit the characters he approves to win full commendation, and to appear on a truly heroic scale. The sinner may be a hero, but the hero is always a kind of failure. That is the other side of the coin, and it may well be that which makes all his characters so human. One may also say that it places his writings into what Frye calls the "low mimetic mode," in which characters are not seen as they are in romance, with supernatural powers or of untainted goodness. Insofar as tradition is concerned, then, Cary belongs in the antiromantic comic tradition which is as much the origin of the novel as is the romance.[41] It is also worth remembering that Cary's double view of his characters follows the path of the greatest example of the genre, *Don Quijote,* a book which has two central characters, one who lives an essentially subjective life, the other a life that looks towards external things.

In *The African Witch,* another interesting pattern of duality connects Judy Coote with Dryas Honeywood. Each is one half of the total woman. The two are obviously opposed types, Judy being rational, intellectual, self-aware, and crippled physically; Dryas is throughout physically graceful, athletic, unable to look into herself, and handicapped by the absence of intellect. Perhaps as a result, Dryas has direct emotional appeal, Judy does not. In the structure of the book as it stands, the Judy-Dryas opposition is fitting. It puts enormous pressure on Rackham. It also places the two girls nicely into the reason-emotion division running throughout the book. That theme is there without them, however, and one girl for Rackham to be jealous over would have been quite enough. On the whole there is no real reason to have both girls, either for the plot or the theme. That there are two seems clearly to be a result of Cary's desire to divide the whole woman, perhaps to show the two sides more clearly, perhaps to remove what excessive authority might stick to a girl who has both beauty and brains, but certainly in line with his habitual pattern of duality.[42]

If Judy is here undercut by Dryas, as Cottee is undercut so much more seriously in *An American Visitor,* Felix Corner is also undercut in *Castle Corner.* Perhaps this suggestion itself makes too much of Felix, since he never has the authority, the general rightness, of such a character as Cottee whom he much resembles. Both are intellectuals, both are aware enough of the general trend of economic development to know about the money to come out of Africa, both are analytical, both go to Africa to get rich, both come from middle-class families who are not quite up to social snuff. Still, Felix is not ever seen with the force of Cottee. If anything, Felix is seen as a comic character, with neither the strengths nor the weaknesses of Cottee. This is probably due to Cary's change of tactics in *Castle Corner,* a book which deals much less directly with ideas than does *An American Visitor* and which therefore had less need of a character who could adequately discuss them. Felix is required not in order to voice specific ideas, but only as an intellectual type.

Nevertheless Felix expresses several points with which Cary agrees. He is especially acute in the discussion of sociology which distracts him from talking business with Benskin (82–87 *CC*). Here Felix argues for a realistic acceptance of the historical force of ideas, and for an acceptance of historical and physical fact. "The lobster," Felix points out, "got stuck because he ran up against the truth—the scientific fact that if you put your skeleton on the outside, you can't develop very far" (85 *CC*). He also sees that there are ideas which are unchanged; ". . . ideas of universal justice and peace and security are the only permanent things in the world . . ." (86 *CC*). Like Cary himself he distinguishes between civilization at any moment—which is "simply floating on a bog" (87 *CC*)—and basic ideas which are "bedrock," and that history in its drive to realize these ideas is moving irreversibly against slavery and for education. He also says that the idea about to come "into the foundations is the abolition of poverty" (87 *CC*), a statement which shocks Slatter but which would only meet with approval from today's warriors on poverty.

In the same way, Felix understands history properly when he sees the necessity of selling Castle Corner, and when he sees the possibilities offered by the expanding African trade.

Nevertheless, Felix is not allowed his moment of triumph. His own venture into Africa is disastrous. His intellect is entirely without practical force, so that he is as incapable of leaving Laka to avoid a foreseeable slave raid as the ignorant pagan natives are (249–56 *CC*). In the same way he is so concerned with the proper education of his son Cleeve that he ignores the topic entirely until he can develop a full system of education for him, an eventuality which does not ever fulfill itself in the book. Even during the conversation, in which he voices Cary's ideas, he is undercut. First of all, he is supposed at the moment to be acting not like an intellectual but rather like a capable businessman who will work up a deal with Benskin. Secondly the narrator quotes "one of his critics"—here again is that typical Cary evasion of authorial responsibility—who rather condescendingly explains Felix's vision of the future golden age of society as

> simply a universal Oxford; a world of quiet colleges, gardens, libraries, parks and streams; peaceful and secure; where the worst conflict would be a college football match or a difference of opinion between rival schools of philosophy, and the limit to freedom would be the same as that which at present restrained dons from murdering each other, stealing each other's wives, levying forces to devastate each other's gardens, or aspiring to the glory of dictatorship—a mere disinclination—a disinclination for these amusements (87 *CC*).

Already, in these early works of Cary, then, can be noticed a dual trend in the narration. On the one hand there is a trend towards omniscience, a trend which establishes that there is a real, knowable world, with definite values. On the other hand there is an abdication of authority by the narrator, suggesting that the world is knowable only to the extent that a specific human being is able to perceive it. In these books Cary also tends to make his narrative speak with three separate voices, a superficially knowing one, a purely sensory one, and a more fully knowing one. Simultaneously Cary establishes a multisided view of reality, resulting partly from the rapid switching of points of view. This multiple view accepts each version of reality from within its own context, but never finally; there is always another view opposed or juxtaposed which undercuts it, or at least appears with equal justification.

In the later trilogies, these trends develop into unmistakable organizing devices. In the first trilogy, where the technique is seen more schematically than in the second, the three separate narrators parallel the three voices of the narrator in the early works. The physical emphasis of Sara suggests the narrating voice which only sees and hears. The historical and political emphasis of Wilcher suggests the narrating voice which has superficial knowledge. The philosophical and aesthetic emphasis of Gulley suggests the narrating voice which has ultimate knowledge. Again, each book from within its own point of view justifies one sinner, so that from within their own contexts Sara, Wilcher, and Gulley all have valid standards. Read together, on the other hand, the three points of view throw questions at each of the narrators, show that each is holding back things either consciously or not, and that they are in fact parts of a larger overreaching pattern of human behavior and of human types. The nester, the creator, the conserver—each is reacting in a human way, one of the human ways, to the reality which controls them all. Each is limited by his isolated experience. Nevertheless, each is living in a world which is "real" and this reality is established by the implied narrator who controls the trilogy as a whole.

## III

The second trilogy—*Prisoner of Grace, Except the Lord,* and *Not Honour More*—is more confusing than the first because its categories are less clear. The framework underneath it, however, is clearly visible. The basic types are still Nina, the nester woman who accepts the situation into which she is thrown and builds her home there, looking always for the physical comforts which include fur coats and well furnished homes; Chester Nimmo, the anarchistic creator always on the brink of going so far with his creativity that he destroys himself and his work, always being reborn, always controlling the rebirth of others; and Jim Latter, the conserver, keeping up the traditional values, sentimental, living largely in the past, always out of touch with the dynamically moving events in the present.

The complicating elements blur this clear pattern. Though Nina is seen as a nester type, she is seen primarily as an individual, as a woman who cannot refuse responsibility. She remains committed to Nimmo largely because he calls on her sense of duty. In this she is like a great many other Cary women; for instance Tanawe in *Aissa Saved* (who tries to protect her cousin),[43] Tabitha in *A Fearful Joy* (who, on the conscious level at least, goes to Bonser and all her adventures because she feels really involved in them, really needed), and Alice in *The Captive and the Free* (who is trapped by the Nimmo-like "missioner," Preedy, because he makes real demands on her).[44] This is the primary point of her book's title, *Prisoner of Grace;* she must respond when needed, whether by Nimmo's selfish ambition, or by Latter's selfish love.[45] That is one reason why the very perceptive Nimmo has such a hold on her with his suggestions that she is distant from him and cannot relate to him. In accusing her of belonging to a social group which is instinctively and unconsciously antithetical to his, he accuses her at the same time of being unable to do anything about it (34 and *passim, P of G*). As a result she tries all the more desperately to prove to him and to herself her ability to relate to him in a personal way, a way which includes, as Nimmo well knows, a good deal of submission. In this reaction she is not entirely unlike Dryas Honeywood whose positive response to Aladai comes also as a result of her sense of responsibility. Because she knows that she does not really want to fulfill her social responsibilities to him, she is much kinder to him than she would otherwise be, and she makes the final effort to warn him, fundamentally, and with a degree of justice, against herself.

In addition, Nina is also the character whose voice, like that of the tourist guide narrator in the early works and like that of Wilcher in the first trilogy, gives the generalized, sociological, historical view of events. Like Wilcher, by the way, she belongs to the upper middle class and is involved with a member of a lower social class. Like Wilcher also she uses a dual view to gain a kind of lack of involvement—she uses the parentheses which Cary found necessary, to allow her to speak the truth about her husband without seeming treacherous; Wilcher jumps back and forth in time between the present and the past. Viewed as form, both are distancing devices. Nina's parentheses do not function only to question Nimmo's sincerity; in a much less mechanical sense they are a clue to what Cary calls her "brackety mind." [46] They help to establish her as a person who can think on different levels at the same time, and incidentally, they also place her in the category which includes Cottee, Felix, Tabitha's son John, and Benjamin—that of the intellectual who is detached and who, though aware, is unable to act on his own knowledge. Thus Nina belongs to more categories than her prototype in the first trilogy, Sara, who in her turn is less fleshed out as a character but who, precisely because she is simpler, certainly appears as more consistent.

Latter, who plays the conservative role that is played in the first trilogy by Wilcher, at the same time has personal traits of Gulley Jimson, as well as of others. His speech pattern has some of the aggressive, clipped quality of Gulley's. If the absence of metaphor and meaningful rhythm indicates that he lacks Gulley's quality of imagination, nonetheless the impatient phrasing of his incomplete sentences indicates a similar quality of force and of full commitment.[47] Never detached, he has in fact the drawback of being committed only to a single idea of duty and honor, or rather, to a single manifestation of that idea. In dress he belongs to one age, unable to see that the general concept of elegance survives in various manifestations as specific styles change. Similarly limited are his attitudes toward honor and justice, which he also wishes to shape into a single abstract mold rather than into a force varying not only with each historical period but also with each individual. In support of his own narrow system, on the other hand, Latter is as imaginative, as forceful, as dynamic, as Gulley. He also shares many traits with Cock

Jarvis, the same kind of man, similarly devoted to duty and honor as well as to clothing which is out of style.[48] He is similar also to Ali, the Waziri's young son in *Aissa Saved,* who has learned the European values of the football field. Ali is, of course, living in a false world, one filled with dreams of glory of his own making and with abstract ideals of justice, but he is still, given the complex conditions of his life, one of the imaginative men of Cary's caste. A further interesting similarity between them is that they both get involved in tasks which come from politicians and which are really impossible to carry out. Ali is asked to stop the riot without any shooting and with only two men. Latter's man, Sergeant Varney, is given the responsibility of keeping order during a strike without being given even as much authority as would come from written orders. As his connection with Ali suggests, the conservative Jim is (within his very severe limitations) a dynamically imaginative man, and thus he fits into more than one category too.

And Nimmo, though primarily the man of imagination, the man who lives by the spirit, is identified by his name as *no one,* and he does finally assume an empty quality in Nina's account.[49] He becomes a voice, an orating voice, behind which lies a sincerity which is only of the spirit, not of the physical world. Like Gulley he is as much destroyer as creator, but there's an important difference. Gulley accedes to the destruction of his art as object; Nimmo eventually destroys himself as object. He remains only his idea of himself, even though that idea is still powerful enough to move others and make them do his will. It is suitable for Gulley as destructive creator to oppose both in his acts and in his language all that is official or pompous, especially the government. Nimmo gains a great deal in complexity because he is the destructive creator who is at the same time an official figure, who is frequently pompous and who is potentially, at least, the head of the government.

Whether or not the view in the second trilogy is wider, it is certainly more complex and the voices the narrators speak in are also not as clearly schematized as those in the first trilogy. Jim Latter's is primarily the voice of the man who sees the objective act, even though he speaks confusingly of his ideals of duty and honour; Nina's is primarily the voice of the woman who sees the general historical and sociological context, even though she is concerned with matters of the body and of the material world in general; Nimmo's is the voice of the man of essential spiritual reality, even though he is contradicting what he is saying at the moment by his crude sexual attacks on Nina.

The complexity in the narrative point of view helps to add a greater irony than is present in the first trilogy. There is much less sympathy for Nina, Jim, and Nimmo than there is for Sara, Wilcher, and Gulley. Nevertheless, each is justified in the sense that he is understood within his own framework. And each is accepted in the sense that he is seen as one necessary part of the total make-up of the social and human situation. The final effect of the trilogy as a whole still suggests an unheard voice—that of the controlling, omniscient narrator who organizes the three separate books as a trilogy—proclaiming a general objective reality within which each of the three individual characters plays his own part.

The tone is considerably more bitter than it was in earlier works. The effect is less sociological and more human than it was. The comedy allows no laughter, or only the ironic laughter which comes from the recognition that people don't know what they're doing. Each of the characters ends up in a state that would normally be considered insane, though it is tempting not to label as insane any character whose motivation has been explained in such clear human terms. Once these developments are granted, it is still proper to say that the over-all pattern of construction of the work has not changed fundamentally from the earlier works. It has, rather, developed in its own direction.

*Mister Johnson* is the work which points to this development most clearly. Here, more than in any of the previous works, the angle of vision stays with the central character.[50] More important, the depth of understanding and insight which the narrator allows himself is perfectly suited for Johnson's book. It allows him to reach as much of the other characters as is necessary. For most of the characters the superficial tone of the narration is in fact quite enough to reach to all the depth there is.[51] At the same time the narration doesn't limit the grasp of the much richer character, Johnson, not, however, because it descends more deeply into Johnson than, say, into Bamu, but rather because it indicates the depth of his imagination which—in spite of the shallowness of his intellect—gives meaning to all of Johnson's actions.

The narrator, certainly not limited to Johnson's awareness, speaks with the multiple voices used by the narrator in the other works. For instance, as the tourist guide the narrator explains that *hamfiss, hamfish,* or *haffice* are the Fada words for office, and that Fada station has been on a temporary site for twenty years (14 *Mr J*). Able to describe superficial motivations, he knows that Rudbeck's interest in building roads is an accidental result of the influence of his first superior in the Service (46 *Mr J*); that Blore is "a deeply sentimental man, a conservative nature" (22 *Mr J*), for whom any exuberance is a threat to his values (24 *Mr J*); that Celia Rudbeck is not alive enough to see the Africa which is before her eyes as a place of sickness and dirt, but sees it instead as "the house of the unspoilt primitive, the simple dwelling-place of unsophisticated virtue" (100 *Mr J*).

As in other works, the narrator frequently dissociates himself from completely authoritative knowledge, as when he says that an old Yoruba trader has "*probably* learned his English at some English mission" (36 *Mr J*) or that Sozy is "*probably* aware of nothing but the need of keeping up with her party and not losing her last place in the world" (178 *Mr J*, my italics).

One character, on the other hand, is presented with extremely unusual narrative authority. This is Ajali, Johnson's friend supposedly, full of *schadenfreude,* not only hoping to see Johnson get into trouble but even helping him into it, and more than a little responsible for setting up the conditions which lead to the murder. His characterization is especially noteworthy because he is the only one of all of

Cary's characters who is explicitly evaluated as bad by the narrator himself. First, Ajali is described as lurking in the store in which he is a clerk "like a scorpion in a crack," with an "insect face" (16 *Mr J*). Later he is shown more fully:

> He is like those others who, vaguely dissatisfied or frightened within themselves, hate everyone else who seems happy or confident in the same circumstances. . . . [He is like others who] have been wasted by boredom and loneliness and self-ishness until they have become a new kind of creature, a sort of subhumanity which can smile and eat and live at a level of corruption and misery which would kill a real human being in a day or two (126 *Mr J*).

Of course there is a kind of excuse for him implied here; the fault is not entirely his. He has been "wasted by boredom and loneliness" and it is one of the points of Cary's books on Africa that the wasting comes about through the sociological problems of a world in transition. Still no one else in Cary is evaluated in this way. And no one else is so clearly and consciously responsible for the downfall of another, for purely gratuitous reasons. Ajali gets nothing out of Johnson's difficulty but the personal satisfaction of seeing him in his difficulties.[52]

It is impossible to say why Cary so unusually evaluates a character here as evil. It may be suggested, however, that the evaluation is entirely in keeping with Johnson's own awareness of Ajali's character: Johnson knows that Ajali "is a spiteful and dangerous man" (60 *Mr J*). He tells Ajali that he is "like a stink bug" and he puts the narrator's own evaluation in his typical metaphorical language:

> You show um a diamond, he tink um broken bottle—you show um a beautiful fine horse, he tink um rock rabbit—you give um bag of gold, he tink um made of snake's head with troat full of yaller poison—you bring um beautiful girl, he say she little dirty goat—he creep on his belly all over everything like house lizard—he say all ting made of dirt (106 *Mr J*).

The knowledge of the narrator then is also the knowledge which Johnson himself has.

The voice of the narrator which reaches most deeply into the book, however, is the voice which reports only what is objectively seen and heard—the voice which reports actions as such, separating them from the human motivations which are underneath them. The voice assumes its great significance because one of the two essential themes of the book deals precisely with the difference between the objective world of action and the subjective world of inner significance or what, for Cary, are spiritual values. Like Gulley's book, *Mister Johnson* is a comedy of the triumph of the inner life over the outer world, in other words, of spiritual subject over impersonal object.

In one of the early sections of the book, for instance, Johnson is running because he is late for work. He is in a panic because he has been warned time and again by Blore, the resident who is his boss and who does not like him, that he must not come late. As he runs, however, his legs take over the action, and the scene is described as if legs have only a general and loose connection with the human being who owns them. "They are full of energy and enjoy cutting capers, until Johnson, feeling their mood of exuberance, begins to enjoy it himself and improve upon it" (19 *Mr J*).

In the last scene in the book there is a very similar division. Johnson has been judged guilty of the murder of Sergeant Gollup and is waiting execution, supposedly by hanging. In spite of the knowledge that he is to die, he feels extraordinarily alive, busy with thoughts of life, without any recrimination, like all of Cary's imaginative men still fully living in the present:

> His mind is full of active invention. He wants to do or say something remarkable, to express his affection for everything and everybody, to perform some extraordinary feat of sympathy and love, which, like a statesman's last words, will have a definite effect on the world.

But at the same time, physically, he is glued to the floor. "His body and legs are not heroic. They are so languid with fear that they seem to be dead already" (225 *Mr J*).

Both at the beginning and at the end, then, Johnson is described in terms of this fundamental division between body and spirit, between man as object and man as subject. And the theme of the book follows this division as well, since it assumes Johnson's sociological problem, that of a man caught in an idea of civilization without having the specific pos-sibilities of civilization open to him. Even more basic is his personal, human problem. Not unlike Gulley's, his idea of reality is continually opposed by his actual needs in the world as it is: he imagines himself an important government official married to a loving, Europeanized wife; this image runs up against the reality of Bamu. He imagines himself a rich man giving joy to his friends and living in a world of parties and largesse; this image runs up against his lack of money. He imagines himself the friend of Rudbeck; this image runs up against the fact of Rudbeck's narrowness and his place in the British administrative officialdom.[53]

The peculiar form of the book is shaped by repeated deflations of Johnson—similar to the deflations of Gulley and similar also to the undercutting of virtually all of Cary's mean-ingful characters—which occur when physical reality confronts Johnson's subjective world. The first example comes after Johnson, imagining and thus creating his love for Bamu, embraces her. A moment later this pagan ferry girl, whom he visualizes as a civilized lady (matching his position as clerk) has stepped out of the ferry and he is drifting terrified down the river, alone. The opposition of the two worlds is repeated frequently; he constantly imagines her as he wants to see his wife, while she lives her own conservative, pagan way of life.[54] Finally at the very end of the book, while he is still imagining her as a good wife, she betrays him by physically maneuvering him so that her brother can knock him over the head and de-liver him to the police for eventual execution.

Johnson's achievement in building the road—one of the important developments of the theme since here the road is an actual translation into physical terms of his spiritual, imaginative power—runs into the deflation he suffers from Tring, and later from Rudbeck himself. His high state at the party he gives while working at Gollup's store runs up against the reality of the colonial situation, and he is fired from his job. His highest state of free imagination comes during his party at the *zungo* after he has been fired by Rudbeck. Significantly, it comes just after the completion of the road, where for once his imaginative and physical capabilities coincided. At his lowest state (from the objective point of view of the world) he forces himself into his highest state of imagination. He fantasizes that the world of reality is an extension of himself. Gollup's store exists for his needs alone. He is king of the whole country. He produces money as if by magic. And it is at this time that he runs across Sergeant Gollup, who carries with him the full weight of the reality represented by the other human beings in the world, by the social system in the world, and by the legal systems, and by the fact of death. Johnson murders; or, in another sense, he creates in his typical manner the condition of his own destruction. The murder, seen in its total context, is the final expression of the contradiction between the internal and external, the subjective and objective; [55] or to put it in terms closer to the narration, as a formal element, between the world as it is seen by the eyes and ears, and the world as it is known by the individual mind.

The world of action, of objective reality, gets its due. Johnson dies. The world of the spirit, of the subjective, triumphs however, not only in the case of Johnson but also in that of Rudbeck. Rudbeck is seen, that is, as more valuable than a man like Tring or Blore.

The victory of the free and subjectively human over the objectively mechanical is a comic victory, and the comic tone is also supported by the shifting in the angle of vision. Significant shifts in viewpoint occur at times of physical violence, when Gollup and Johnson fight, later when Johnson kills the trader, and when Rudbeck shoots Johnson.

The conflicts and friendships between Johnson and the two white men are obviously not simply matters of personal relationship between the people involved, but deal with the total relationship of white to native, and enter into the sociological complexity which was emphasized in all of Cary's previous books and which always remains for Cary the situation within which individuals live. Perhaps in order to avoid having to treat fully how racial feelings involve the deepest sensibilities of individuals (a subject he didn't fully explore even when he got close to it, as in the incident between Aladai and Rackham), Cary deals with the hitting of Johnson by Gollup and the hitting of Gollup by Johnson entirely externally, even though the second incident is important enough to get Johnson fired.

The fight serves as one of the deflations of Johnson. It is also a triumph of the objective, the impersonal, the external, over the subjective. Still the externalized quality of the description—Gollup's "right fist," for instance, "clasps and unclasps several times as if feebly rehearsing a series of knockouts" (139 *Mr J*)—moves the emphasis away from the meaning of the action, as well as from the social evil which lies behind it. The narration does not remove these unpleasant aspects, but it removes primary attention from them; it allows the comic element to be maintained without fundamental falsification.

In both of the other two scenes of violence, the angle of vision shifts at the critical moment away from the one who commits the action. For instance, although the narrative has followed Johnson throughout the chapter in which the murder occurs (185–97 *Mr J*), it moves away from him in his actual trip to the store. Instead it follows first Ajali, and then Sergeant Gollup himself, who is entirely ignorant of whether there has been any thievery and who thus has no understanding of the meaning of the event. The description of the killing itself is given briefly and externally, mirroring Gollup's own unawareness:

> At once something long and dark, with a bright flash before it, seems to uncoil from the floor, straight at his breast. He fires and feels a thump on his bare chest. Then his legs

give way and he says in a surprised voice, " 'Ere, 'ere. Wot you playing at?" He's dead (197 *Mr J*).

In the case of Rudbeck's shooting of Johnson, such aware-ness that there is, is given to Johnson, whose conscious thoughts are directed in gratitude to Rudbeck:

> All the force of his spirit is concentrated in gratitude and triumphant devotion; he is calling all the world to admit that there is no god like his god. He bursts out aloud "Oh Lawd, I tank you for my frien' Mister Rudbeck—de bigges' heart in de worl'."

The act itself, committed after all by Rudbeck, is de-scribed without any internal content whatsoever: "Rudbeck leans through the door, aims the carbine at the back of the boy's head and blows his brains out. Then he turns and hands it back to the sentry" (225 *Mr J*). There follows an examina-tion of Rudbeck's conscience after the act.[56] But this consists of only two sentences and doesn't go very deep: "He is sur-prised at himself, but he doesn't feel any violent reaction. He is not overwhelmed with horror. On the contrary, he feels a peculiar relief and escape, like a man who, after a severe bilious attack, has just been sick" (248 *Mr J*).

In both cases the evasion of internal content in the crucial acts serves to create in part what may be a necessary ambiguity. Johnson, after all, ought to be seen as both guilty and not guilty at the same time. Like every significant human act in Cary, the murder he commits is the result of the forces acting on him, which he is totally powerless to control; however, at the same time the murder is equally the result of his own free decision. The evasion is also in line with Cary's persistent refusal to show fundamental knowledge of the actual process of decision. Primarily, however, the evasion here serves to maintain the comic tone. " 'Ere, 'ere. Wot you playing at," emphasizes the comedy of the mechanical man; it is not quite the same as a murder. Johnson's thanks to Rudbeck for shoot-ing him suggest the comedy which is the triumph of spirit over death. That is not quite the same as a cold-blooded shoot-ing done as a favor to an associate.

In contrast, the scene in which Johnson is ready to murder Rudbeck's boy, Jamesu, but does not, is seen from Johnson's own point of view, without any apology. Johnson even thinks at the time that he ought to have killed him; "Why you no kill him, you fool chile? Now he go talk" (75 *Mr J*). Since there is no actual murder in this case, some content can be given to the event without breaking the comic effect. Johnson's resolution appears not so much as a potentially evil act as a willingness to act out fully his imagination.

One more point ought to be made about *Mister Johnson,* and that is that the book, more than the others about Africa, emphasizes the human over the sociological, the personal over the social. The difference is readily seen in the difference between two very similar relationships—that between Bamu and Johnson as compared with that between Uli and his wife in *The African Witch.* Uli's attempt to introduce his wife to European ways leads him nearly to disaster. When he takes her face to face, in defiance of the taboo, she rejects him and he rejects himself. He is lost socially, belonging neither to the world of the missionaries to which he runs, nor to the world of the tribe whose taboo he has violated. For a while he turns into a case history of what happens to a tribesman, imaginative enough to be willing to try change but not strong enough to stand against the full force of his tribal background. He is clearly a sociological example.

When Johnson tries to force his vision of European culture onto Bamu, the scene itself is comic, partly because of the practical way in which the problem is objectified. He tries to force her physically into a pair of drawers, while she is physically, and successfully, rejecting this attempt to "civilize" her. The relationship between them, while a result of sociological differences, is yet seen fundamentally as a human relationship, an effect stemming not only from the difference between Uli and Johnson, but also from the quieter narrative tone and from the greater reality of detail in *Mister Johnson.* The relationship between Bamu and Johnson is more domestic, just as the entire action of *Mister Johnson,* even including the murder itself, is on a lower, quieter, more individual and domestic level than any of the other African books. *Mister Johnson* does not deal with revolutions, with large-scale riots, with large political questions, but only with the problems and reactions of some individuals. These individuals are closely connected to the larger sociological issues dealt with in the other works, but still the tone is quieter, and the focus more personal.

In this way, too, *Mister Johnson* points to the future. All the important characters function in more than one way. Sozy (bare impulse to survive at the lowest level); Salé (hanger-on of a corrupt court); Bamu (a case study of the conservative pagan); Waziri (the servant of a feudal court); Rudbeck (the man caught in the "conditions of the service"); Tring (the fussy administrator miscast in the role of a man on the spot)—they all have an allegorical role and they are also all related to their larger circumstances. But none of them is seen in detail in his sociological situation. Each is seen in the book as relating directly to Johnson and his individual case; each is seen also in an individual way. This mixture of the individual and the type, of the personal and the sociological, of focus on one specific case while pointing out its reverberations in history and society—this is the mixture which later typifies the two trilogies. The interest is as large as it was in the past. But *Castle Corner* and *Mister Johnson* are two opposites: *Castle Corner* points in the direction of large sociological works, showing distinctly large forces and showing these forces through individuals; *Mister Johnson* points in the direction of more narrowly focused personal works, though showing these individuals as affected by their sociological context. *Castle Corner* is the end, more or less, of one direction. *Mister Johnson* is the beginning of another.

# *Notes*

[1] This development is by no means in a straight line. *The Moonlight*, 1946, and *A Fearful Joy*, 1949, though appearing between the two trilogies,

do not have a first person narrator. Neither does *The Captive and the Free*, the work Cary was working on at the time of his death. This novel, however, was originally intended to be a trilogy on the general lines of the first two. See Hoffman, *Joyce Cary*, p. 159.

2 For the relation between form and psychology (of the audience, not the hero) see Kenneth Burke, "Psychology and Form," in his *Counter-statement* (University of Chicago Press, 1951), pp. 29–44.

For an annotated listing of works on the point of view in fiction, see the bibliography in Wayne C. Booth, *The Rhetoric of Fiction* (University of Chicago Press, 1961), especially section II, pp. 405–18. The book itself is a thorough study of this and related matters of fictional technique.

3 See, for instance, Erich Auerbach, *Mimesis* (Garden City: Doubleday, 1957), pp. 463–88, esp. p. 472.

4 It is useful to consider the matter of the narrator's authority in the light of Dorothy Van Ghent's statement that the novel "proceeds by hypothesis." *The English Novel: Form and Function* (New York: Rinehart, 1953), p. 4. The hypothesis is in great part established by the narrator's assumptions.

5 *Mimesis*, pp. 1–20.

6 *Ibid.*, p. 19.

7 The *Odyssey*, translated by E. V. Rieu (Baltimore: Penguin Books, 1953), p. 50.

8 *Mimesis*, p. 8.

9 Mahood considers the mosquitoes here as proof of the blind injustice of events, since both Bradgate and the Carrs overlook their existence, p. 188.

10 Tabitha in *A Fearful Joy* and Rozzie in *Herself Surprised* are two other such excessive characters.

11 She thus becomes the first of several major Cary characters to face death with laughter; Gulley and Tabitha are others.

12 Hoffman shows that the invasion was part of the early conception of the opening scene, although complicating elements, for instance, the conflict between the rational Mr. Carr and his emotional wife, were developed in subsequent drafts. *Joyce Cary*, p. 9.

13 The riot can be considered as directed by the historical situation which is its cause and which has been detailed in the earlier sections. In any more personal sense than that, however, it is undirected.

14 The same device is used by Cary in *The African Witch* where Ibu runs away from the ju-ju compound and the view shifts with her first to the no-man's-land of Musa's playground and then to the palace. It is used once more in *Castle Corner* when Bridget Foy is sent out of the besieged hut and leads the view into the castle.

15 At this time Obai is still on Bewsher's side; his running along with Bewsher here is in strong contrast with his killing of Bewsher later. There he is opposed to Bewsher in theory and, physically, stands his ground against him.

¹⁶ See Mahood, p. 137.

¹⁷ Cf. Cary's explicitly stated belief, in agreement with Cottee, that a carefully developed policy is needed. See for instance, *Case,* p. 33, where he says that the necessary reorganization of Africa requires "a very definite idea of what kind of result is wanted."

¹⁸ Cary almost wistfully considers the possibility of controlling the development of an African tribe by cutting it off completely from outside contacts. He rejects this Bewsher-like notion, just as Cottee does, but not because it is an undesirable one, only because it is impossible. See *Case,* p. 40. This alone suggests strongly that Wright is mistaken when he sees Bewsher as without any disinterested benevolence, and only as a megalomaniac who wants to subdue and outsmart the natives. Wright, pp. 79–80.

¹⁹ He is one of the few such in Cary, and probably the only one to have success, though his success may be illusive; after all he is not seen throughout his life. Other Cary intellectuals are Tabitha's son John, who turns repeatedly away from the possibility of achievement and who eventually dies because he is submissive to his modern, aggressive wife; Edward Wilcher, the aesthetic intellectual who briefly has enormous success in politics before he withdraws; Jim Latter's brother, a cultured, refined, scholarly man who leaves quietly after a threat from Nimmo; and Felix Corner, who is discussed in some detail later. All refuse the opportunity to do anything, partly because they're not sure exactly what has value.

²⁰ Cf. the similar point made by Bulteel in *Mister Johnson,* p. 167.

²¹ Cf. Cary's statement that, "primitive societies are not anarchic. They are closely governed by social and religious sanctions." *Power,* p. 56.

²² Cf. Cary's Preface to the Carfax edition of *The Moonlight,* pp. 6–8.

²³ This discussion of history is based on an anecdote of Cottee's about a lady in a Russian story who tried to protect her beautiful china from drunken soldiers. The soldiers, assuming that the cabinets must be full of money, smashed everything to pieces and tortured the old lady to make her confess where the wealth really was. "What did she expect?" asks Cottee in commentary, adding that she did not realize that "beauty would not perish with her Sèvres" (235 *Am V*). Hoffman criticizes Cottee for not understanding that the pieces were unique and therefore · aluable in themselves. *Joyce Cary,* p. 24. This is clearly not valid. That Cottee does grasp the point is what makes the story apposite. Cottee thinks the lady wrong not because she tried to save her china, but rather because she did not understand the facts of life, just as Marie does not understand when she keeps the gun from Bewsher. The more general point is developed in the first trilogy, where Gulley accepts, unwillingly enough it is true, the destruction of individual paintings because art will always go on.

²⁴ She also accuses him of hypocrisy, but that accusation may well be traced to her feelings for Bewsher, Cottee's opponent, and to her own past relations with Cottee. Similarly his attitude to Marie may be partly due to a mixture of jealousy and sour grapes.

²⁵ Another such type is Grain, "the tea man," of the short story "A Mysterious Affair," in *Spring Song and Other Stories* (New York: Harper,

1960), pp. 92–105. Grain "is never in doubt about anything because he never sees the inside of anything; he's a closed file. Neither is he the man, like poor old Ned, to take a chance, to bet his life, to follow his dream," p. 105. If Grain, like Cottee, is right without being liked or having effect, note also such Cary characters as Schlemm and Dryas who may not be right but who are liked and who are effective. Cf. the narrator's belief that Dryas had influence over Aladai because of her "fine character. . . . Character always made itself *felt*" (296 *Af W*).

26 There may be something here of the traditional humor which is directed at novices and expresses itself in hazings and ribbings. It may also have something to do with Cary's ironic view of himself as a young man first entering the Service. That he did see himself in this ironic way is clear from the letters and drawings he sent home from Africa (see Mahood, *passim*), and from his African reminiscences. See, for instance, "Africa Yesterday: One Ruler's Burden" and "Christmas in Africa," both reprinted in *Case*. Furthermore, considering Cary's tendency towards doubling characters and noting especially that he split himself into an older and a younger brother in *House of Children*—see the Preface to the Carfax edition—it is not at all impossible that Cary may have been thinking of Gore and Cottee as two parts of his younger self. Another example of Cary's tendency to doubled characters is one of Cary's illustrations, described by George Garrett as "a two headed monster, one face a weeping cuckold with horns, the other a wildly grinning laurelled satyr, set together like Siamese twins. . . ." "The Major Poetry of Joyce Cary," p. 253. The illustration seems also pertinent to a consideration of Chester Nimmo.

27 For Cary's awareness of the need to develop the ideas necessary for his fiction see, for instance, "The Way a Novel Gets Written," *Harper's Magazine*, CC (February, 1950), 87–93. About his conscious removal of explicit ideas from his novels, Mahood says, "a study of his manuscripts shows that again and again a directly explanatory passage, either in the author's own words or in the speech of a character, is replaced in the revision by new actions, sometimes performed by characters invented for the purpose," p. 188. Hoffman's study of the manuscripts shows the same procedure again and again.

28 Hoffman believes that "Cottee's analysis [of Marie and Bewsher] serves the same function as Marlow's analysis of Lord Jim in Conrad's work." *Joyce Cary*, p. 23. There are other similarities: Bewsher's leap, though it has an entirely different function, still recalls Jim's. There seems also a general desire to raise Bewsher's significance by making him the subject of speculation by others, also like Jim. Marie's images of life as a ship also have a Conradian look.

29 This kind of drawing together of themes in Cary has not generally been acknowledged. It might be noted also that in the same section Rackham also uses a suggestive image to describe Dryas' mixture of physical and moral strength with intellectual weakness: "She'll never break, never go to bits. But she might sink bodily into the mud. . . . Yes, that's what it floats on, all that sentimental sixth—form culture. Slush, a crocodile swamp" (267 *Af W*). Rackham uses the same image to characterize her brother's lack of freedom: "His will was the servant of nature, the crocodile in the swamp"

(193 *Af W*). Later, this image is embodied by Osi, a girl very similar to Dryas in her lack of rational control, who walks into the swamp to sacrifice herself literally to the ju-ju crocodile (293 *Af W*).

[30] My italics. The angle of vision here may be Fisk's, as it has been throughout the chapter, or it may have temporarily shifted away from him; it is impossible to tell from the passage itself.

Bloom, rather offhandedly, speaks of Cary's "reticent omniscience" in discussing the limited knowledge of the narration. *Indeterminate World*, p. 44.

[31] That Cary was aware, at least in general, of the need to work out a relationship between the formal elements of the work and the characters' self-awareness is seen by his defense of the present tense in *Mister Johnson*, in the Preface to the Carfax edition, pp. 7–10.

[32] This sort of attempt is never repeated in Cary's published fiction. He is, however, repeatedly concerned to show that religion is an observable fact, as here Judy, following her discussion with Schlemm, learns that "the spirit can be projected" (346 *Af W*). The novel also shows, in a rationalistic way this time, that ju-ju witches have the effect they claim to have, apparently through psychosomatic influence. The problem of the Master of the Horse, whose arm swells after his run-in with Elizabeth, is an example. In addition there may be just a slight hint that Christianity works in a very practical way, when Aladai seems to be miraculously saved even though a spear is thrust directly into his chest. The spear is stopped by a book in his pocket, and in view of the context, it may be significant that the book is a Christian prayer book, not, for example, *Notable Sex Crimes in the Nineteenth Century*, another book known to be in Aladai's library.

[33] See the Preface to the Carfax edition of *Castle Corner* (6–8).

[34] This does not mean that her intelligence is not functioning. It is she, for instance, who calls attention to the difference between Aladai's regal bearing and his unsuitable Western clothing, especially noted in the riding up of his trousers legs. It is the reader, though, who makes the connection between this incident and the discussion earlier about "trousered apes."

[35] Hoffman, *Joyce Cary*, p. 32.

[36] Henri Bergson, *Laughter*, in *Comedy*, ed. Wylie Sypher (Garden City: Doubleday Anchor, 1956), p. 79.

[37] *Ibid.*, p. 97.

[38] *Ibid.*, p. 84; the italics are Bergson's.

[39] But note that though Honeywood is shown as a puppet, he does not seem at all comic. Perhaps this is because he is not so much shown as described. Cf. also the comic polo and bagatelle games, both mechanical applications of rules in a context where they do not fully apply.

[40] *Comedy*, p. 220. There is no reason here to detail disagreements among various theories of comedy. In any case, Bergson's view can be seen as a special one, valid for certain kinds of comedy, while Frye's view is larger, though not necessarily complete either.

41 Cf. Fielding's antiromance definition of the comic as the exposure of vanity and hypocrisy in his Preface to *Joseph Andrews* (New York: Norton, 1958), pp. XXIII–XXXIV.

42 Robin Sant and Harry Dawbarn in *The Moonlight* are examples of a division of the male into the physical and the intellectual.

43 Tanawe "had learned to be dutiful and to serve a common purpose. She knew that it was shameful to fail in one's duty" (66 *AS*). Earlier she feels her responsibility when she feels that, "this was not a game, it was something important" (34 *AS*).

44 Alice says, "I wasn't precocious—he hurt me—and I wasn't mad about him—I thought he needed me—it's what he said" (162 *C and F*).

45 Those who accuse Cary in general and Nina in particular of moral irresponsibility seem especially susceptible to the error of assuming that Nina is tied to Chester because she believes this to be her debt to a great public figure. See, for instance, Bloom, pp. 109, 176; and Giles Mitchell, "Joyce Cary's *Prisoner of Grace*," *Modern Fiction Studies*, IX (1963), p. 264. But cf. Cary's statement that "Nina was held to her husband by her sense that he was on the whole a good man." Preface to Carfax edition of *Prisoner of Grace*, p. 6.

46 *Ibid.*, p. 8.

47 Bloom thinks that Latter's language "verges on a kind of headlong military illiteracy." *Joyce Cary*, p. 179. Another critic thinks his "staccato telegraphic style perfectly suited to Latter's desperate shut-in feeling." Elizabeth R. Bettman, "Joyce Cary and the Problem of Political Morality," *Antioch Review*, XVII (1957), p. 271.

48 More interesting even than Cock Jarvis' appearance in *Castle Corner*, is the unpublished novel which bears his name. The best description of this work is in Mahood, where attention is also called to the relationship between Jarvis and Latter. See *Joyce Cary's Africa*, pp. 96–104, esp. p. 99, where Cary is quoted describing *Cock Jarvis* as "a study of an honest man who didn't understand what politics was all about."

49 Latter's name suggests his dislocation from the time he lives in, while the duplication of n's in Nina's name suggests both softness and childishness.

50 This may be part of what Cary had in mind when he called Johnson the "artist of his own joyful tale," a statement open to the interpretation that Johnson tells his own story. See the Preface to the Carfax edition of *Castle Corner*, p. 8.

51 In suggesting that the cause of the shallow view in this book is the present tense, Cary seems to be claiming a great deal too much credit for a grammatical device. Preface to the Carfax edition of *Mister Johnson*, pp. 7–10.

52 Cf. for instance another, Morton, the tough boy in *Charley Is My Darling*, who seems at first to be, like Ajali, only a villain. He attacks children without reason, he does his best to drown Charley, and he submits as ungraciously to Charley's leadership as Ajali does to Johnson's. Morton is explicitly regenerated by being explained in human terms, while he is

in the middle of one of his dirtiest tricks. The reasons for his wrong behavior are his own feelings of rejection and wickedness, caused by his
humped back, and his mother's spoiling of him. All he really wants, the
narrator explains further, is to be accepted by a girl for himself (271–78
*Charley*). No one else comes close to being evil in this way in any of
Cary's other books. Nimmo, it must be remembered, is seen as evil only by
a bitter enemy.

[53] With this lack of reality cf. Cary's statement that, "false ideas are
especially dangerous to their holders. . . . A man who believes that his
nation is the greatest in the world may be confronted with the facts, like
defeat or a low standard of living. He has then the choice of inventing
some fantasy to explain the facts away or despising facts altogether and
committing himself to fantasy." *Power in Men*, p. 222.

[54] Cary sees the problem of Johnson's marriage as typical. Village
heads, court clerks, and other such Europeanized natives are often forced
to marry primitive girls, who then bring up their children the same way,
he says, since women are more conservative than men. *Case*, p. 106.

[55] It is difficult to see exactly what Wright means when he says that
"his last great act is the greatest act of all, that of murder. . . ." *Joyce Cary*,
p. 85. Johnson is, like Kurtz in *Heart of Darkness*, free of normal human
restraints, and he is in a high state of imagination. But the murder itself
is a kind of intended accident. There is no greatness in the act at all.

[56] Cary was very much aware of what he was doing here. In earlier
versions the shooting was seen from Rudbeck's point of view, and Rudbeck's decision to do the shooting was shown with some detail. See Mahood,
pp. 185–86, and Hoffman, *Joyce Cary*, p. 40.

# 3. The Official and the Personal

There are two other dimensions to the division in Cary's novels between the outer and the inner, the objective and the subjective, terms which are closely connected with what has been called the eternal subject matter of the novel: the conflict between appearance and reality.[1] One of these dimensions is Cary's insistence on always contrasting the abstraction with what he considers the real, the specifically human, the individual.[2] Another is his related practice of opposing the truth as seen by official sources, with the reality of events as they occurred to living individual human beings, both in their acts and in their consciousnesses.

The ineffectiveness of abstractions is pointed out clearly in the inability of Cary's intellectuals to act effectively or wholeheartedly in the world. Beyond this, however, Cary further denies that abstractions such as goodness, justice, and mercy have any existence except for the strange, the often dangerous and contradictory existence they have in real people in real situations. An example of Cary's attitude is the sermon preached in *An American Visitor* by Dobson in praise of love, after Bewsher has almost miraculously escaped from a dangerous and seemingly hopeless trap by the Birri. The sermon is an important one in the book in many ways, since it exposes precisely that thinking which makes Marie decide not to give Bewsher his gun when he needs it. Indeed it is the sermon which she hears from her sickbed that converts her. Bewsher attends the service largely because, though his own religion has none of the formal convictions of Christianity, he thoroughly enjoys such things. The scene itself is split throughout between the generalizing, abstracting sermon of the minister and the practical thoughts of the man who lived through the experience discussed in the sermon. As such the scene has a clear framework. The basic question is phrased by Bewsher himself: "What would Dobson make of the combination of luck and bush-craft that had got him out of Paré" (217 *Am V*). That the discussion is one to be taken seriously is made obvious by Bewsher's assurance that Dobson always "put up a first-class show, good plausible argument on reasonable premises. He never played tricks with texts or hit below the belt with sentiment. He was as honest a preacher as he was a man" (217 *Am V*).

Dobson begins with a general point: that justice, mercy, and love are facts of experience. To prove that "angels are stronger than guns," he cites the case of the abolition of slavery by the force of ideas of justice, not by physical force.[3] Dobson then uses the example of Bewsher himself as a proof of the power of love:

> It is certain as the sunrise that he owes his life to the fact that I have stated, the strong repugnance of any man, however fierce, ignorant and deceived, to kill any unarmed man who comes to him in friendship. And that fact, a scientific fact of experience, is proof alone that there is a god in the world, a god whose spirit is attested by the fact not only of our inner experience, but as clear in operation to our eyes and to our critical judgment as these rays of light which fall upon this desk from the open sky. God is love and love is strong (219–20 *Am V*).[4]

All the time Dobson is speaking, Bewsher is thinking of the practical problems of his administration of the Birri. He wonders whether it would be "a good plan to hang the Nok murderers from their own roof trees as soon as he reached the place or bring them through Birri in chains?" (218 *Am V*). He thinks that after his system of federation for the Birri is accomplished he will be able to bring in the traders for the money they will bring in with them. Ironically, he thinks also that missions, such as Dobson's, will have to be postponed, perhaps as much as twenty years, until he has developed a full creed based on the present ju-ju (220 *Am V*).

The difference between Dobson's attitude and Bewsher's is not emphasized strongly here simply in order to develop the irony of a clergyman making more of a case than the man involved, or to show the irony of a man who is not aware that his plans and his actions deny the faith he thinks he has. That irony is there, but a more important idea is there too. After all, Bewsher does have love for the Birri, and Bewsher did survive, and Bewsher did go unarmed to meet vastly superior force. Dobson is not wrong in that sense. His mistake is only in creating an abstraction, and Marie compounds the mistake by believing that the abstraction can actually affect such realities as spears.[5] Bewsher survived in fact, not because of any influence of love, but rather because the Birri couldn't decide exactly how he ought to be killed and how his body ought to be disposed of (166 *Am V*). Previously his life had been saved—"several hundred times already"—because Bewsher was so odd a specimen that no native could know, "what would happen if he were killed. What would his spirit do?" (71 *Am V*). Bewsher is a living example of the power of love. It gives him a meaningful life. It brings Marie to a fuller life. It brings the Birri to a greater state of freedom, even though that freedom takes extremely unpleasant forms. Most of all it gives him subjectively a meaningful life and projects him into a level of existence at which heroism is possible. But he is also an example of the failure of love when it is seen as bare abstraction, or when the easy assumption is made that love brings automatic good. The truth is that his love has brought results that he did not expect: violence and murder, a nationalism destructive rather than creative, and disorder rather than the orderly progress he had planned.

In a scene handled very similarly, Cary counterposes another sermon dealing abstractly with love with an example of love as it is lived by real individuals. This scene is in *The*

*Horse's Mouth,* when Gulley attends a meeting of Plant's and hears a sermon on love (73–86, Chapter 15, *HM*).[6] While the lecturer, Professor Ponting, talks abstractly of love as the basis of the good life, Gulley and Sara sitting on a decrepit couch and drinking Plant's beer, act out what real love is, awkward, selfish, tough.[7] It should be noted that while the love described here is extremely crude, it nevertheless still has creative force.

Since Cary thinks of human beings as belonging to fundamental types, his various characters may even be thought of as being specific, and therefore "real," examples of abstractions. Thus Gulley can be considered a specific individual example of the abstract creative type and Sara a specific example of the nester type. The many repetitions of the same type—for instance, Aissa, Gulley, Johnson, Bewsher are all creators, while Jim Latter, Cock Jarvis, Zeggi, Stoker are all conservative soldiers—indicates only that the general character trait finds innumerable workings out in practice.[8]

The error in abstract thinking is basically a philosophical one, assuming as it does that ideas or emotions can exist without human beings to think or feel them. The error of the official way of thinking is that it omits the practical details which make a situation real.[9] In a sense this is the problem in all the books. The second trilogy can be seen, for instance, as an attempt by Jim Latter to present the specific, measurable, objective facts—facts that would stand up in a court of law, against the abstract truths of Nimmo and the official truths of Nina.[10]

This trilogy, the most complex of Cary's works in many ways, allows no easy, simple resolution to the opposition of different kinds of truth. It leaves the theme ambiguously open, suggesting in the long run that both ways are wrong as well as right. The point can be seen in one of the critical incidents of *Not Honour More,* the trial of special officer Maufe, who had been accused of using unnecessary violence in arresting a communist leader during a strike. Jim, who headed the specials, believes that Maufe is being railroaded by Nimmo and Nina. When Maufe is convicted—partly because during her testimony in court Nina evades giving specific informa-

tion about a visit she made to one of the crucial witnesses—
and when Jim discovers through letters that she and Nimmo
did in fact do what they could to work against Maufe, Jim
kills Nina because "the rottenness has gone too far" (221
*NHM*). The case makes all the headlines but becomes mis-
represented, as Jim thinks, into a "common adultery case"
(222 *NHM*).

The incident has multiple suggestions. It suggests first
that while the papers have the facts all wrong, the trial, an
official attempt to reach the true facts, has the case at least
partly wrong. There is no suggestion, however, that Jim's
version of the facts is right. Even though Nimmo has an interest in seeing that Maufe gets convicted, the testimony of
Bell—which Nina helped to discredit because of her evasion—
may still have been prejudiced, consciously or unconsciously.
And even if it had not been, Maufe might still have used bad
judgment and unnecessary force in making the arrest. Jim is
not in any position to know these facts more definitely than
anyone else.

What is clear is that while Jim is looking for the facts,
and makes it his stated intent to give them, Nimmo, in his
approach generally, is after facts of a very different nature. He
talks of the large, abstract forces moving the country—of
love and grace. Both approaches are extended beyond their
possibilities by the two men. Jim insanely overvalues the external act, and murders for the sake of his truth. Nimmo's
abstraction leads him to lose touch with the real world so much
that he brutally attacks Nina while talking of love.

The African books contain the opposition between the
official version of events and their real truth in a much more
simple way. In a sense all these novels correct the public, news-
paper-sponsored notion of what the situation in Africa is like.
In addition to correcting, they also substantiate—in the sense
of adding substance to—the abstract terms used for Africa:
Empire, indirect rule, nationalism, progress, and so on. And
all of the African novels also show the division which exists
between the administration's abilities and the real need, between its intentions and its acts, between what it thinks it is

doing and what it is really doing. Throughout, there is an implied criticism of the lack of clear plan and direction of the Foreign Service; the fundamental effect, however, is not critical but rather descriptive and individual men are not seen doing the right or the wrong thing but doing what their own situation compels.

In *Aissa Saved,* Bradgate, the resident, is quite unaware of what is really going on in the minds of such people as Aissa, or in the minds of the more conservative natives, or even for that matter of the white missionaries, the Carrs. As a result, while he spends his time with his favorite occupation of building bridges, corruption and bribery, not to mention riots and ju-ju deaths, take place around him.[11] Nevertheless, Bradgate is shown to be a decent man, working hard to do a good job. If he works physically, utterly without a sense of dignity, that is because he is dedicated to accomplishing things; primarily he is an example of a local official caught between the administration which frustrates his desire to build things by withholding the money, and the emir, who frustrates him by his conservatism (70–83 and *passim AS*). In order to get anything accomplished at all he has to move carefully in both areas, keeping both sides satisfied according to their own peculiar standards. He is essentially a politician working in a political framework, as he recalls when he pays the bribe demanded by one of the badly Europeanized natives, simply to get the job done (82 *AS*).[12]

In the same way Gore, in *An American Visitor,* works as effectively as he can in a difficult political situation growing out of the disparate demands of the various groups in Africa. It is by the nature of the situation—as much as by the nature of his character—that he becomes a man of compromise. Another such man is Burwash, the resident in *The African Witch,* who seems particularly incapable of achievement in a book which ends with seeming defeat for all the forces of progress. But even he is seen as working in a framework within which his behavior and attitudes are acceptable. Burwash tries mostly to glide gracefully out of trouble, and his social skill at ending discussions, commented on by Rackham and Marie, is a symptom of this. As one consequence he spends a good deal of his time—three hours a day (184 *Af W*)—composing his letters and reports with what seems like excessive care. His conversations with his assistant, Fisk, allow Cary to show the details of Burwash's practice. Amongst other corrections, Burwash changes a clear statement like, "The trade situation is bad, and is getting worse," to an officialese: "The trade situation is unfavourable, and shows signs of further deterioration, due to the new railway" (185 *Af W*). He similarly explains the destruction of some correspondence by ants as "a hiatus in the correspondence" (185 *Af W*).

Destructive to the wholesomeness of the language as this is, and silly as it makes Burwash sound, still there is some reason for Burwash's excessive care. His job, after all, is not to write good prose, or even to be intelligent. His job is a political one which calls for an achievement which can become possible only if others involved can be fooled, forced, or convinced to cooperate. In an early experience, for instance, Burwash found himself unable to help thousands of starving farmers because he phrased a sentence badly in a report, and his opponent in the case seized the opening.[13] As Burwash believes,

in a world where it is impossible for the rulers to have personal contact with the ruled, and government must willy-nilly depend chiefly for its data on reports and discussions by letter, the wording of reports and letters is an important matter. Real things—the lives, happiness, destinies of living people—depended quite as much on the literary skill as on the political ability of an officer (184 *Af W*).

It seems impossible to argue with this view, and nowhere does Cary do so.

This is not to deny Burwash's ineffectiveness and ignorance. He is a man utterly lacking in the imagination necessary to enter into understanding of another, the kind of imagination which allows Fisk to relate to Aladai.[14] He is completely mistaken in his inability to recognize Aladai's obvious superiority to the other contenders for the emirate. He is just as mistaken in his evaluations of the political details of the campaign, not recognizing Elizabeth's women's revolt for what it is, not recognizing Aladai's actual position for what it is, and of course not understanding anything at all of the ju-ju situation which Schlemm fights against so valiantly. Throughout everything, he is concerned for his own position in the Service. He points out, to Fisk again, that

> What one has to remember is that after a really serious crisis—that is, the very kind that is most likely to cause an inexperienced officer to lose his head—there is bound to be an enquiry; and nothing makes a worse effect in an enquiry than evidence showing that heads have been lost (278 *Af W*).[15]

Perhaps the point is simply that Burwash is miscast in his role; a generally decent, kindly man, he simply does not have the quality of imagination necessary to do the job in which he has been placed.[16]

A problem shared by all of the British administrators in Africa is their lack of general direction, compounded by a similar lack of awareness of their basic political and religious principles. In *The African Witch* the point is made not only by Burwash's general unawareness of wider issues, but also by Rackham's inability to look into himself. In *Aissa Saved*, Bradgate feels vaguely guilty because although he knows himself to be unselfish, he also knows that he could not answer such basic questions as "What are you really doing in Yanrin? What are you driving at?" (113 *AS*).

In *Mister Johnson* the same problem is the subject of a curiously uncompleted discussion between Rudbeck and Bulteel:

> "Don't you believe in the native civilization?"
> "Well, how would you like it yourself?" Bulteel smiles at him sideways with a kind of twinkle.
> "Then you think it will go to pieces?"
> "Yes, I think so, if it hasn't gone already."
> "But what's going to happen then? Are we going to give

them any new civilization, or simply let them slide down-hill?"

"No idea," Bulteel says cheerfully. . . .

"I suppose one mustn't talk about a plan," Rudbeck says.

"Oh, no, no, no. They'll take you for a Bolshy" (167 *Mr J*).

In *An American Visitor,* the point is emphasized more than in any of the other novels because of the conflict of ideas be-tween Cottee, Marie, and Bewsher. While Marie plumps at first for no government at all, and Bewsher for a carefully controlled, isolated development, Cottee makes the point that, "We haven't got a system at all—no sort of principles. None of the people we send out have the faintest idea of what they're for." And when Gore comes to the defense of the system by appealing to the nonintervening principles of in-direct rule, Cottee insists that nonintervention is "not a prin-ciple at all—it's just lack of intelligence" (98 *Am V*).[17]

An image which more or less sums up the actual situa-tion of the administrators in Africa is the bagatelle game or-ganized by Captain Rubin—one of the most decent men in *The African Witch,* but also one of the men most removed from events, in the way typical to many of Cary's soldiers—during the middle of difficulties which are already violent and which become more violent shortly afterwards. All kinds of ironies surround the incident, so close to fiddling while Rome burns. Yet while the irony is recognized, even by Burwash himself, the players nevertheless take the game seriously. The peculiarity of the game lies in the absence of a firm board on which to play; the board, "changed its shape from day to day; sometimes in the course of a game or the roll of a ball" (281 *Af W*). This image may well stand for the refusal of the African situation to fit the rules which so many of the whites, like human beings everywhere, have come to consider uni-versal and unchangeable. In fact, in this sense, the African situation is not essentially different from the situation in England, as the historical books and the trilogies show; though no situation is ever static, the change in England is nevertheless more orderly than in Africa.[18] Change in Africa can be as violent and surprising as the accident which causes a winning ball to miss its mark:

> the whole board, before the eyes of everybody, was seen to open from end to end. The side on the left of the crack rose; the right-hand side sank down, leaving a gap of more than two inches, through which the winning ball shot into space (283 *Af W*).

Like life itself, the table on which the board is placed "was flexible . . . all its hinges had free motion in all directions" (283 *Af W*). It is only the freest person, the most adjustable, the one who has both the fullest understanding of basic principles and the greatest ability to apply them as conditions change, who can successfully play this game. Gulley, Nimmo, Tabitha, are some of those who fit into this category. So does Johnson.

But of course success is not final, and only exists on one side. The free, adjusting man also runs into obstinate facts, such as the inflexible ground under the flexible table (to carry on the metaphor of the bagatelle game) not to mention the conflicting desires of other human beings—the opponents at the game.

In both *Aissa Saved* and *The African Witch* official inquiries oppose the reality of specific events, much as the trial does in *Not Honour More*. While the latter book indicates that every effort at finding the truth gets caught up in the problem of the subjective mind of the man who testifies, in *Aissa Saved* and *The African Witch* this problem is not an issue. The inquiries in these two books suggest only the more limited point that the official truth is necessarily a misrepresentation of the actual truth. Political considerations, the ignorance of officials, and the abstracting tendency of official language all obscure the truth, which is only to be found in the actual experience—subjective as well as objective—of human beings.

In *Aissa Saved* the inquiry exonerates everyone, praising "the Carrs for their magnificent work in Shibi, Bradgate for the notable progress of the last five years in Yanrin, the native administration for its statesmanlike coolness and moderation in a dangerous crisis" (158 *AS*). Except for the coolness and moderation of the native administration—who were moderate only in the sense that they did not know what to do, and took action only when Ali suggested his own impossible task—this evaluation is no more false than it is true; it simply omits everything that is significant.

The report in *The African Witch* does not contain any general allocation of praise and blame, since the inquiry was not formal but only a report on the women's strike. Beginning with a brief history of other women's strikes to serve as comparisons, the quoted section of the report calls attention to Elizabeth's moderating influence. This, too, is neither false nor true; it simply is not relevant to the facts. The phrase used by the report to deal with her abduction, her poisoning, her discovery by Ibu, her Amazon-like working off of her anger gives the clue to what's missing: the report speaks of "her unfortunate absence," for experience that belongs to romance.

It is in *Mister Johnson,* however, that the opposition between the official and the real is most significant; this issue is central in the book, merging with the division between the inner (the subjective life), and the outer (the objective life). In the first place, Johnson's problem is caused by the dislocated social structure into which he has been thrown and the dislocation is caused by the British presence in Africa. Not only are the British there almost all public officials, but they all insist on an official, impersonal relationship with the natives.[19] The theme becomes most explicit at the end when Rudbeck in his decision to shoot Johnson finally breaks through the official requirements into a real, human relationship. Just before he does the shooting, he tries to escape from his sense of responsibility by preparing for the hanging which is at the extremity of the official, nonhuman relation between state and individual. He "carries out his usual office routine with great exactness and even exaggerated precision" (213 *Mr J*). He finally goes to his task of weighing Johnson saying, " 'Oh, very well,' in the tone of one who says, 'You've asked for it.' " (213 *Mr J*). The actual weighing, in the absence of a real scale, is done by using silver coins, the weight of which is known, and this too may point to the nonhuman element of the case, where the nexus is one of cash rather than of sympathy.[20]

Rudbeck has a vague awareness of the role officialism plays in the life of Johnson, and in a final conversation he is trying to assess his own degree of identification with Johnson. He doesn't charge himself with the responsibility for Johnson's fate, but he knows he has had something to do with it, and he thinks back to a report he wrote about Johnson: "That report of mine—I don't know if I was quite fair to you" (223 *Mr J*). Johnson reassures Rudbeck, with his charming inability to feel joy unless he is also giving it. But in fact the report has had something to do with Johnson's end. This report is another one of those examples of a report which, as Burwash fears, may actually lead to harm for a human being. Rudbeck's problem then is not that he didn't phrase the report correctly so much as it is that he has no capacity to do paper work at all. He hates paper work, he does not look into his feelings—which in themselves are honest—and so he really doesn't know what to say about Johnson. As a result, he falls back on a casual evaluation made by Blore (who hates Johnson because of his sense of life, among other things) and writes, "Willing, but careless. Has little idea of filing" (62 *Mr J*). Like the other official reports, this is not false, but certainly not true either. One immediate result is that Johnson does not get an advance in pay he needed. A more serious result comes later, when Tring, Rudbeck's replacement, has found out about Rudbeck's improper financial handling of funds to build his road. One of the people he reports is Johnson who is then discharged, partly, as Tring later says, because "Both Mr. Blore and Mr. Rudbeck gave you very unfavourable reports . . ." (115 *Mr J*).

Tring himself is an embodiment of officialdom, with seemingly no human quality at all, and who seems to personify all the rigid elements of what Bulteel calls "Service conditions" (168 *Mr J*). He seems so official, so unwilling to adjust regulations to real human beings, that even his superior becomes cautious. Bulteel thinks, but is careful not to say, "Damn it, I'd better be careful. . . . He may report me next" (115 *Mr J*). It comes as no surprise therefore that Tring is also an expert at writing reports which will "catch the right eye at the right time" (142 *Mr J*). By the time he leaves he has finished a special report on "The Organization of a Bush Office" and on "Native Prison Organization," and has also prepared a lecture on "A New Life for the African Delinquent" (141–42 *Mr. J*). This last article is especially ironic in view of his lack of sympathy with the only African delinquent he has actually known, but his other reports, based on actual achievements though they are, have no greater value. His achievements are the sort to be quoted and reprinted; they stand in contrast to Rudbeck's officially improper building of the road, which gets him into official difficulties, but which has the real effect of increasing trade, freedom, and, of course, trouble.[21] Tring's contrast to Rudbeck stands parallel to the contrast between Johnson and the clerk Montagu, who is seen with any fullness only after Rudbeck shoots Johnson and who is, "neatly dressed, perfectly correct, an excellent clerk who never makes a mistake" (226 *Mr J*). He is certainly there to serve as a standard of the mechanical, the nonhuman, the objective, and incidentally as something by which to measure Johnson's final achievement and Rudbeck's final leap from the nonhuman and official into the personally meaningful.[22]

Johnson is continually in trouble with officialdom, with the rules which he does not fully understand, and with official reports. His difficulties with money are a natural outgrowth of his personality, which demands continually that he go beyond the reasonable bounds, and that he express his limitless imagination in forms which strain finite reality. But it is also an expression of his improper relation to the civilization which has brought a commercial way of life to Africa, along with the official laws that accompany it. Thus he does not fully understand his guilt in extorting money from the laborers who get their pay from him, as clerk (31 *Mr J*). Though he reacts indignantly when the Waziri suggests that he steal official reports for him, he is forced to steal anyway by a trap operated by this same law. The Waziri, though he is in conflict with the creatively free Johnson, is also a free man, as can be seen from his willingness to visit Johnson in the latrine, without regard to his official dignity. His freedom is of a type other than Johnson's, however. It is the freedom of a man whose only concern is to get the job done; he is unfettered by pride, personal feelings, friendship, and all such personal matters.[23] His freedom thus is not the sort which would urge him to relate personally or fully. As a matter of fact, he stands as an opposite in type of personality and use of power to Johnson; he is a man with great potential whose fulfillment is limited by the sociological situation.

Johnson's ridiculous lack of skill at filing and at arithmetic are further examples of his inability to fit into his official role as a clerk. He is the man who is officially classified but who does not have the actual skills to go along with his classification. Johnson's case represents basic failure on the part of the British in Africa. They have placed him in a position of danger without giving him the resources to deal with it. They have made him want a clerk's way of life and have given him a love for British things so intense that he naturally speaks of England as "home." They have given him the title "clerk," but they have not really given him the education, the ethics, or the grasp of European life which he requires to live properly as a clerk.

Of course his dislocation is a strength in Johnson too; it is partly because he does not belong to any official structure that he can suggest to Rudbeck the false vouchers and the misuse of appropriations which finally get the road built. Strength and weakness are so merged in Johnson's character that it is impossible to divide them.

For a man like Johnson, even more than for others, a formal and official attempt to get at the truth is certainly not going to work, and thus the trial is not going to discover the objective truth of the murder. The investigation leads nowhere except to Rudbeck's vain attempt at explaining Johnson's official position. One of the comic effects of this book is indeed Rudbeck's attempts to make an official trial out of it, while his official language contrasts with Johnson's attempts to talk to a friend.

The opposition between the official and the real (that is, the human) then goes to the very core of *Mister Johnson*, and if the ending does not satisfy the kind of insight and understanding of the colonial situation which some may demand,[24] it still comes, formally, with a comic triumph. But in another sense the ending leads to a fundamental irony, since each of Johnson's successes leads him to catastrophe. His human relationship with Rudbeck brings him death. The other human (or partly human) relationship he has had with a white man, Sergeant Gollup, gets him beaten up and then fired in this colonial world where human values are not allowed. His friendships with Ajali and his love for Bamu lead to his capture. And his relationship to the Waziri also brings him a beating, so violent that he needs a bigger party than ever to make up for it, besides more money, that medium of the official world which then leads indirectly to his death. The official structure is not alive, not real. Johnson's kind of personal and creative freedom does not necessarily lead to kindness, to happiness, or in any simple sense to the good. It does lead to greater achievement and thus to greater freedom. In *Mister Johnson* it creates the road, but though this road is surely an important achievement, it leads Johnson to his death, and since the creatively free man has no caution it leads there quickly.

# *Notes*

1 "The work of the novel . . . is the investigation of reality and illusion," according to Lionel Trilling, "Art and Fortune," in *The Liberal Imagination* (New York: Doubleday Anchor, 1953), p. 247. In another essay, "Manners, Morals and the Novel," Trilling uses the phrase, "the old opposition between reality and appearance." *Ibid.*, p. 202.

2 About politics, Cary says, for instance, the first question is, "how does this affect the real men on the ground, the people in their private lives,"

*Case,* p. 12, and he adds that "abstraction" has led to "The greatest political . . . mistakes." *Case,* p. 130. Similarly, the major point of *Power in Men* is an attempt to define freedom in a way that will emphasize its specific effect on specific individuals.

3 Felix Corner, though he paradoxically defends slavery in its own context, has a similar view without the religious terminology (84–88 *CC*).

4 In his *Paris Review* interview, Cary said nearly the same thing. There he couples his belief in unselfish beauty with his belief in God. "How can one explain the existence of personal feelings, love and beauty in nature, unless a person, God, is there? He's there as much as hydrogen gas. He is a fact of experience." John Burrows and Alexander Hamilton, "The Art of Fiction VII: Joyce Cary," *Paris Review,* No. 7 (Fall-Winter 1954–1955), 68. It can be further noted that Dobson's sermon is another example of Cary's insistence that no abstraction can exist except in a mind. If love exists in many men and at various times, beyond the specific experience of individual human beings, Dobson seems to assume, then that must prove a being outside of history, or God, in whose mind the love exists. Cary never explains why love and beauty cannot be accidental results of psychological patterns in all human beings, transmitted genetically, as it were, in the same way by which the body structure is transmitted, and valued as good only by the same individuals.

5 Cf. Cary's statement in *Power in Men:* "Love truly overcomes evil. This is probably the most important truth of religion. But it does not overcome all evil, as religion itself insists. Hatred, intolerance, spite, greed—all these need the discipline of the will. Injustice, disease, inequality of powers belong to the nature of reality and the perpetual conflict of good and evil within that structure." Pp. 155–56.

6 Plant fits into the pattern which opposes the abstract to the real. His position on the side of abstraction is seen when he first praises the stars and then looks up quickly, according to Gulley, "to make sure there were such things still to be seen" (69 *HM*).

7 The same scene, with interesting variations, is the subject of the early version known as "The Old Strife at Plant's," in *Harper's Magazine,* CCI (August, 1950), 80–96. A similar juxtaposition is seen in Chapter 14 of *Prisoner of Grace* (44–47) where Nina's "real" reaction is juxtaposed to Chester's abstract prayer. The passage also fills in the "real" details of the abstract term, "conversion."

8 As Wright points out, presumably speaking of Cary's characters, "Cary's range is severely limited." *Joyce Cary,* p. 72.

9 "Africa Yesterday: One Ruler's Burden," in *Case,* gives an interesting parallel example of the problem of presenting information officially. The report of an officer on the spot suggesting a new road to increase business is translated into entirely different terms by the chain of communication. Pp. 208–209. The same point is made from the point of view of the man at the top in *A Fearful Joy,* where John translates reports into readable form for his stepfather James Gollan.

10 That Latter hides facts himself in spite of his repeated intention to get at them only shows the difficulty of reaching the truth.

The closest approach to truth in Cary is in fact through art, which "alone can communicate the feeling as well as the fact," that is, the subjective as well as the objective element of experience. *Art and Reality* (New York: Harper, 1958), p. 31.

Note also that while Tabitha despairs of truth in a historical text, the version given in her book, *A Fearful Joy*, is implicitly a true one.

[11] A typical Cary touch, between irony and applause, has a steel bridge going up as one of the by-products of the riot, along with two new Christian missions and an increase in the money allotted to education, which will allow five students from Yanrin "to learn football, cricket, and the multiplication tables" (159 *AS*). Civilization progresses in its own way.

[12] Cf. Cary's description of the difficulties white officials in Africa have in getting the facts they need. *Britain and West Africa*, in *Case*, pp. 183–84.

[13] Interestingly the name of the opponent was Cock Jarvis.

[14] But note that Fisk's official report, about Osi, is also wrong (139 *Af W*). The official in Cary is never right.

[15] This reference to lost heads points ironically to Schlemm's fate. In contrast to Burwash, who always plays safe, Schlemm, who risks his life for his beliefs, literally loses his head, which is then used by Coker in the ju-ju ceremony which costs Osi her life (292 *Af W*).

[16] Cary distinguishes between two different kinds of skills: "The general staff deals with figures, papers, maps; the subaltern deals with men, events, mud, rivers, and mountains. The first needs great powers of concentration and foresight; the second, a genius for improvisation and quick decision." *Case*, p. 84. Burwash seems to have the skills of the first group while in the position of the second.

[17] In *The Case for African Freedom* Cary describes all four points of view mentioned here. Indirect rule, working by suggestion rather than by openly using power, and by supporting the structure of government already existing, has the advantage of letting progress come naturally and of being easy to administer. See esp. Chapter 6, "Political: Direct and Indirect Rule," pp. 49–60. On the other hand, a serious failure of indirect rule has been its lack of direction. Apparently choosing his language carefully and moderating his statements so that his point would be more acceptable to the administrators he was trying to influence, Cary asks whether an inherent defect of indirect rule is not "its lack of direction. For it has, according to modern views, no object or purpose at all." P. 59. Thus both Cottee's and Gore's views find support in Cary. On the other hand, both Marie's views and Bewsher's find a negative reception. Bewsher's attempt to cut the natives off from contact simply won't work. Marie's view is given special prominence because Cary considers her anarchist sentimentalism especially dangerous and perhaps also because, as he confesses, he shared many of its points as a young man. Pp. 33–42.

[18] As Cary points out in an entirely different context, the change which brought motorized cars to England was accepted by carters who were used to change and to whom change came as part of a vast changing pattern through which they had lived. In Africa such change is completely revo-

lutionàry, unaccompanied by the vast social and educational changes which might lead to easier and more organic acceptance.

19 Cf. Cary's belief that Africans, educated Africans as well, require a more personal relationship than Europeans in order to function effectively. *Case*, p. 36.

20 Cf. *Power in Men*, where Cary, discussing the Kantian requirement of submission to the truth even when a murderer asks where his victim is hiding, says: "A man has no right to conceive of himself as the machine tool of a principle; he cannot get rid of the responsibility of freedom." P. 69. This injunction is acted out by Rudbeck.

21 In one of his notebooks, Cary described Tring as "a rat but a clean rat." Quoted in Mahood, p. 176. Apparently Cary connected the sound of Tring's name with the rigidity of his character. The ideologically rigid labor leader in *Except the Lord* is called Ping, while the inflexible doctor in "Government Baby," *Spring Song*, pp. 221–39, is called Bing. Bing is also the name of the estate agent who fires Nimmo because of his opposition to Nimmo's antiwar views.

22 Note should be taken that the last sentence of the book describes Rudbeck as "growing *ever more free* in the inspiration which seems already his own idea." My italics.

23 Gollan in *A Fearful Joy*, Bradgate in *Aissa Saved*, even Gulley Jimson are of the same type.

24 Arnold Kettle feels that the ending of *Mister Johnson* is blemished by Cary's lack of awareness of the social issues. *Introduction to the English Novel*, Vol. 2, pp. 183–84.

# 4. History
# and Irony

Cary's works exhibit a continuing interest in history and historical development. *The Moonlight* and *A Fearful Joy* are both works whose primary purpose is to trace the changes brought by time into the sociological context and thus into the attitudes and reactions of individuals. This is also expressed through major themes of both trilogies and of *Castle Corner,* and is more than hinted at in other works. Superficially viewed, the works seem to make the point that history is a process of decay, with the passing of time bringing only the dissolution of an orderly past and the loss of firm moral standards. Perhaps such a view even corresponds to an attitude held by Cary himself. The full effect of the theme, however, is to show that history is always in a state of being created and that thus each moment contains the possibilities of either triumph or defeat. No moment is ever fixed, and none ever limits the individual's potential achievement. The standard of universal order which seems to belong to the past, therefore, is not a real one, but only one which the future superimposes on its memory of what has gone.

For Cary one standard nonetheless does exist, and it is the eternal, unchanging basic pattern of humanity. No individual is ever the same as another, but none is ever totally different from his fellows. Both the differences and the similarities—appearing as a fixed constant underneath changing events and under all the differences cloaking various societies—make for a strand of irony which insistently appears in most of Cary's works.

In *The Moonlight,* Ella Venn, the spinster who is determined in her own way to marry off her daughter Amanda, has put up for sale the house and its furnishings, which she has just inherited. The auctioneer, taking advantage of the prestige and interest that the sale of the Venn estate is sure to stimulate, brings into the house some other things, crude and tasteless, to sell along with the Venn property. Ella sits for a while on a couch and gazes at a statue of Phryne, both of which have just been brought in by the workmen. Suddenly she makes a discovery:

> Her eyes grew large, her lips parted; she gave a little cry and half started up. "Why—where is this?" She looked round at the unfamiliar objects which had so silently gathered about her, as at the substance of a dream, in which her past life was as fantastic as the extraordinary carpet, the strange chairs and tables, the enigmatic Phryne (134 *Moonlight*).

The immediate reference of this image lies in Ella's past, and relates to her discovery that far from being an innocent victim of circumstance and a tender heart, as she has typically pretended to be, she has actually helped to create the love affair which gave her an illegitimate daughter. The presence of the statue Phryne (the Greek *hetaera* who served as the model for Praxiteles' Aphrodite and who was acquitted in court after having been exhibited naked) suggests her part in the relationship and may even suggest that far from being an idealized Aphrodite she has always been a real life Phryne.

A little later, another discovery is made by Ella's daughter Amanda, who has trouble falling asleep in her room, which is packed full of the furniture reserved by Ella from the general sale:

> The red-plush padded chair with its sloping shoulders on which a tattered anti-macassar hung like a fichu, seemed to hold out its fat stumpy arms, not with comical welcome, but with an animal sensuality, gross, sheeplike; the bedside cupboards seemed like grotesque priapic monuments; the grey

headless Mary Jane in the corner with its absurd tortured waist, its forced-out chest and stomach, became the characteristic form of that for which it stood as representative Victorian woman, a sensual victim and machine, a fleshly device for the production and nourishment of other little lumps of flesh, a creature as little free or noble as the segment of a tapeworm; and beyond, in the corner among the confused heap, one saw a huge sideboard carved with grapes, a washstand holding apart its thick crooked legs, a hat-stand flourishing horns against the dim portrait of which nothing could be seen but a white neck rising from a low-cut frock; and draped behind, the great plush curtains drooping with crimson folds like the walls of some immense womb (149-50 *Moonlight*).

The immediate reference of this image lies in Amanda's discovery of her physical nature and of her role in life as a woman, and more specifically in her reaction to Ella's attempts to marry her off at all costs to a neighbor farmer. Looking at the house from outside a few minutes later, after having gone out in an attempt to relax, she thinks: "The very house is like a woman in a low frock, sitting here waiting to be admired, half undressed to excite some man" (150 *Moonlight*).

Quite aside from the immediate context of the two images, they are typical of Cary in that they use the house and its furnishings to represent an era and also in that they present that era apparently in a state of decline from a more stable past.[1] Throughout the book the Venn villa suggests the stability of the old order, of family life, of accepted values, and of happiness, if only because it is the place where all the meaningful events of the past have occurred. As the intellectual nephew Robin says—like other Cary intellectuals he is right without being a valued person—"this place is above fashion. It's like a shrine. . . . Life is different here, Aunty. One *feels* different. One realizes that people can live with *dignity*" (111 *Moonlight*). Into this worthy and stable house comes the comparatively shoddy, the second hand, the tasteless, as represented by the furnishings brought into the house. The stable old order is shown to dissolve under the pressure of time itself.

*Castle Corner* as a book was built on this very foundation, showing the changing history of the Corner family set against the changing history of England, with the castle itself serving as the device to hold the book together.[2] Not only do the main characters continually revolve around the house, but their ability to maintain it is also a major issue in the book, measuring as it does their ability to survive in a changing society. They do maintain the house at the end, but the loss of stability is obvious. The opening scene of the book shows old John Corner, who is characterized by the word "father." The opening words of the book, spoken by him are, "And now to God the Father . . ." and he obviously believes in God as the father of creation, the king as father of his people, and sees himself both as father of his family and of the tenants whose landlord he is. In his firmness with the tenants, his sense of duty up to the moment of his death, and his unquestioned ruling of his family, he is a personification of stability. At the end of the book the castle still belongs to the Corners, but the conditions have changed enormously. The Corners own the house only because a piece of accidental kindness, which depended on the flip of a coin, gave their worthless investment in Africa some value (408 *CC*). While the elder Corner son, Felix, is in Africa, no doubt thinking of his philosophy while tickling the enormous Dinah, the inheritor of the castle, John Chass, practices his special art of hospitality by throwing parties and spending money at a rate which is sure to bring on another crisis.

In *To Be a Pilgrim*, Wilcher's country home, Tolbrook, like Castle Corner, becomes a central motif, and possession of the house is a major question. Tolbrook, like Castle Corner, represents a standard of taste and value, and like the Venn villa its breaking up suggests the dissolution of the firm standard of the past. Nowhere is the point made so clearly as in the scene which places a threshing machine among the cupids of its famed and beautiful saloon.

The book which shows most definitely the dissolution

resulting from history is *The Moonlight,* perhaps the bleakest of any of Cary's published works. The book makes its historical points not by progressing in time, as *Castle Corner* and *A Fearful Joy* do, but rather by juxtaposing the past with the present in the memory of Ella, a lady of seventy-four at the time the book begins. The moral standard is developed in the character of her older sister Rose, who has the high Victorian sense of moral responsibility, accompanied by an equal sense of personal freedom. As a result she gains her way continuously by moral bullying, to which Ella continually submits but which she also continually tries to evade. Both, for instance, seem to accept Ruskin's aesthetic views, which "exactly answered the hungry demand of such as Rose, eager, warm-hearted, for beauty which they could permit themselves to love, for an aesthetic which enabled them to delight in form and colour, and feel at the same time that they were not idly wasting time upon frivolity and self-indulgence" (72 *Moonlight*). Only Rose, however, is able to maintain her allegiance to duty while influenced by Ruskin. Ella pretends she does, but her lack of ultimate sincerity becomes clear when her aesthetic interest is translated into sympathy for a Pater-like poet, Geoffrey Tew, who believes in art for art's sake, and with whom she would have run away if Rose had not gotten rid of him.

Rose is in love with Professor Groom, a scientist whose strength lies more in the force of his moral ideas than in his scientific knowledge, but in contrast to Ella she gives him up for the sake of her duty to her father, who has been widowed and whose hedonism certainly requires her services.[3] What's more, Rose has enough of a sense of duty to force her younger sister Bessie to accept Groom when she might not want to, and to go back to him when she wants to run away.[4] In almost direct opposition to this, Ella allows herself to be seduced by Groom's assistant, Ernest Cranage.

Ella's illegitimate daughter Amanda, brought up by Bessie as her own, repeats Ella's history in the sense that she, too, becomes pregnant without marriage, by Harry Dawbarn, a physical, practical, down-to-earth farmer, who treats both sheep and women with a rough kind of knowledgeability. But there is a major difference between the mother's case and the daughter's. Ella's notions of marriage, including "sensations of exaltations, sacrifice, danger, mortality and pride" (18 *Moonlight*), are contrasted with Amanda's notions of sex as a Pavlovian reflex (16 *Moonlight*) and as a swindle by nature to continue the species (91–92 *Moonlight*).

The present seems in every sense to be smaller and less valuable than the past. Amanda's present-day intellectual friend, Robin, is less creative than her mother's intellectual friend, Cranage. At least Cranage produced Amanda. Robin doesn't even get as far as adultery. Iris, the modern girl who fits perfectly into the early twentieth century and who becomes an intellectual who rejects sex completely, is less of a personage than her mother, Bessie, who ran away from her husband because of an initial disgust with sex (49–50, 272–73 *Moonlight*). Another of Bessie's children, Dorothy, has the bossiness of her aunt Rose, but shares none of her standards or convictions. A son, Bertie, is a hedonist, as his grandfather was, but much more crudely and less intelligently; his interest in his grandfather's library extends apparently only to "certain French editions de luxe, with illustrations" (275 *Moonlight*).

Although it is true that this book is shaped by the juxtaposition of the present with the past, the past only seems to be a firm standard. Eventually the past is seen as not firm at all but rather full of individual variations, which extend from Rose's full commitment to Ella's half-conscious evasions, and which include also the father's irresponsible hedonism. The constant in this change is the actual nature of woman, with her biological drive and her sexual function. Using this constant as a standard by which to measure periods, the book shows the past not only as changing into the present but as decaying into it; the Victorian world, personified in Rose, is more in accord with woman's nature than the early twentieth-century one. The book ends with Amanda pregnant and alone by choice determined to bring up her child. She has refused to marry Dawbarn, though he gets to farm the land which

Ella has bought with the money she got for the villa, and at her last meeting with her cousin Robin, "Their lips did not give anything but merely asked a question" (314 *Moonlight*). She does her boring job conscientiously, but her feeling is

> one of pity and emptiness; not self-pity, but a universal pity as for all the loss, the frustration, the waste, in the world, and the emptiness was the shell of this pity. It lodged in a vacuum, without object, without will or hope or love. It was merely a vast still grief (315 *Moonlight*).

Her overwhelming sense of loss is not effectively counteracted by the suggestion of a miracle, when Amanda asks herself, "But do miracles happen? It will be interesting to see" (315 *Moonlight*).

It is to be noted with particular care that the sense of loss so clearly present in *The Moonlight*—the sense that history is degeneration—does not correspond to Cary's notion of history as expressed elsewhere. Rather, his works make the point repeatedly that the constants in human life—sincerity, devotion, sex, reason, for instance—find different kinds of expression in every age. The specific forms are always in dissolution and new ones are always in the state of being created. Both the creator, Gulley Jimson, who believes that art will always go on no matter what the specific form, and the intellectual, Cottee, who insists that beauty will be recreated even though a specific kind of beautiful china is destroyed, agree on this point.[5] In *A Fearful Joy*, which covers roughly the same period of time, and which also shows the relations between different historical periods Cary is less concerned with evaluating periods or people and more with showing how basic character asserts itself in different individuals living in different times in history.[6] The book outlines a number of historical periods from about 1880 to shortly after the Second World War. It begins by setting as the social standard the bourgeois world in which Tabitha Baskett, the central character, originates. Her father, an old Whig physician who enjoys his drink and his risqué stories, is already out of date in his own time. His more capable son, Harry, grows into a successful doctor, busy making money, submissive to his wife, and without any ideas or principles of action beyond that. When he retires from his work, he has nothing left except his submissiveness.

Tabitha, whose chief characteristic is energy and who is always looking for excitement—the first paragraph shows her setting the nursery curtains afire, laughing and shouting to excess (9 *FJ*)—repeatedly escapes from this dull environment. The image which best sums up her relationship to the ordinary life she so often rejects comes at the end of the book, when her brother Harry, retired and without active interest, sits in his chair,

> apparently in deep meditation, until a drop of rain on the window makes him jump . . . or the whisk of Tabitha's skirt rouses him, and he cries irritably, "Sit down, Tibby. Nan's quite right, you are a regular fidget. But you never could settle to anything from a child" (336 *FJ*).

The opposition between excitement and boredom forms a major theme in the book. It is the excitement represented by Bonser, an irrepressible confidence man, war profiteer, and hedonist, which makes her run away with him from her dull home as a young girl, and to run back to him even when she knows all his lies and faults. She feels, for instance, at one point, "that if she had never met Bonser her life would be inconceivably flat and stupid" (29 *FJ*). The same sense of excitement, mixed with a typical womanly concern to lead a meaningful life as a mother, causes her also to accept the various forms of her never quite respectable life. She rejects her one major chance to assume the role of a respectable woman of her class, because the nice young man who offers her marriage is dull (110 *FJ*).

The book strongly tends to characterize the late nineteenth century in England as largely a search to escape boredom. "It is boredom that has broken the immense fortress of the old Christian society," says the narrator himself (77 *FJ*). Both world wars are popular because they permit a breaking out, an exciting assertion of the self (212, 314 *FJ*).

After leaving her traditional world through the back door

of Bonser's underworld, Tabitha leads the book first into the period of the aesthetic nineties. On one side this section serves as a picture of the period, focusing on an aesthetic *Yellow Book*-like magazine, *The Bankside,* and peopled with such characters as the Beardsley-like artist Dobey, the Francis Thompson-like poet Boole, and the Frank Harris-like editor Manklow. More significantly for the shape of the book as a whole, the section shows Tabitha in the middle of a social and literary activity especially designed to break up the traditional conventions, becoming very much the traditional mother in bringing up her son John. Her brusque motherliness apparently also accounts for her conquest of Sturges, the millionaire who subsidizes *The Bankside* and whose need for a cold, bustling, superiority she satisfies without being aware of what she is doing.[7]

Her acceptance of the feminine responsibility is an example of human nature making itself felt in a new historical context. Although her child is illegitimate, although she is an exile from traditional society and helps to voice the *fin de siècle* attack on it, although she is in the position of the demimondaine, she becomes the protective mother, conventional in all her attitudes, bribing her child with affection (89 *FJ*), putting his comfort high above the needs of the great poet Boole (101 *FJ*), and turning to prayers for his spiritual needs (90 *FJ*). As one of the hangers-on of the group says, "Funny . . . how these fillies run true to type. Here's our little girlie setting out to make her by-blow into a bishop, whether he likes it or not" (94 *FJ*).

Her behavior here is paralleled almost exactly by that of her son's daughter, Nancy, who also becomes a dedicated and protective mother both to her child and her husband, after a youth wild by traditional standards. Nancy is the product of another generation, and another group of values, values which have in fact been helped into being by the forces which Tabitha supported but which afterwards disturb her enormously when she sees them in action.

Not only has Tabitha helped the aesthetic and intellectual attack on the Victorian principles through her *Bank-*

*side* involvement. She has also been involved in the economic and industrial attack on the past through her marriage to James Gollan, an industrial leader who helps to develop the motor car and make it a major factor of life in the post-war period.[8] The changes in transportation, through which Gollan helps to produce major social changes, become a major theme in the book. Bonser, with his urge for profit and for excitement also has great interest in cars. He first is involved in a rubber combine which tries to do business with Gollan, and then is among the first to foresee the change cars will bring to the hotel business (253 *FJ*). He installs Tabitha in a roadside hotel which offers dancing for the young (who of course get there by cars) and which reflects part of the vast social change that permits a much more open and casual disregard of traditional sexual mores than in the past. Here again Tabitha has helped to separate the present from the past, by doing her share to produce the social circumstances which bring her granddaughter Nancy to her hotel with young men, who are also, as Tabitha discovers with dismay, her lovers.

Tabitha brought up her son John during the dissolution of Victorianism. This dissolution led directly to the between-the-wars modernism in which John's daughter Nancy was brought up. It is during the next period (the dissolution of modernism after the Second World War) that Nancy returns to the duties and responsibilities of motherhood. Her mother, Kit, who objected to "impulse and instinct and sex" (231 *FJ*), after producing Nancy apparently by accident, had refused her any signs of affection, any religious training, or any real system of rules by which to orient her life. While Nancy's early wildness cannot be seen as inevitable, it certainly can be expected. However it is entirely unexpected that she should throw herself fully into her husband's needs, though the only desirable quality he has is his Bonser-like excitement, his tense connection to life. Like Ella Venn, who sells everything for Amanda's marriage in *The Moonlight,* Tabitha sells every-thing for the sake of making Nancy's marriage successful, and though her hope of remaining with the household is not fulfilled, the marriage does turn out successful. This is another way of saying that basic human character has, in a new period, asserted itself in a new form. And it is no wonder that, in contrast to the stoic and grudging acceptance of life by a young pregnant girl at the end of *The Moonlight*, *A Fearful Joy* ends with the wild excitement of children in a park and with the sigh of an old dying woman, ". . . of gratitude, of happiness" (388 *FJ*).

The two trilogies have an element of historical interest also, both moving from the late nineteenth century to the period of the Second World War. This element is most prominent in *To Be a Pilgrim*, where there is also a sense of decay in history, although Wilcher makes a strong attempt to accept the changes which come with time and which themselves bring in the future.

The sense of the destruction of beauty is strong in this book. Tolbrook, which serves as a metaphor for the beauty and stability of the past, is sacrificed to the pressing life of the farm and the needs of the young couple, Robert and Ann. In a parallel way the children of Wilcher's sister, Lucy, and of his brothers Edward and Bill, are lesser versions of their parents. Robert, Lucy's son, has her stubbornness, but only a little of her sense of excitement and life. In place of her commitment to religion and duty, he has a significantly lower dedication to farming according to modern methods. In place of her running away to the nonconformist religious leader Brown, he casually fathers children from two girls. The same reduction of intensity stands between him and his father, who also has several women. John, Bill's son, has his father's easy acceptance of the rules by which society lives. In Bill this meant being a disciplined soldier, making a success of marriage, and accepting death without objecting.[9] For John this means acceptance of postwar cynicism and its lack of values, refusal (or inability) to work at anything he holds meaningful, and submission to an unfaithful wife. Ann, Edward's daughter, has her father's interest in abstract ideas and also his lack of passion. But while his failure of faith came only after a good deal of success as a politician, her failure begins with her childhood. Her success, on the other hand, is limited to having her child, and sharing Robert with another woman. The children are like their parents, but as Wilcher says of the close similarity in the appearance of Ann and Edward, the children's features seem to be those of the parents with a veil blurring the clear features of the past (13 *TB P*).

The relationship between past and present is speeded up in a filmlike image which merges the two boating scenes. In the contemporary scene, actually viewed by Wilcher, the boat is leaky, the party is small, consisting of Robert, Ann, and his farm-girl mistress; but, in the scene he remembers of the past, the boats are gay, the party is large and elegant (137–39 *TB P*).

The loss produced by time in this book, similar to that in *The Moonlight,* is contrasted by the constant recreation of the spirit, similar to that of *A Fearful Joy.* The division entirely suits the dichotomy seen in Wilcher, who alternates between the love of material things (that of the conservative holding on to the remembered glories of the past) and the love of the spirit (that of the creator open to the changing life of the future). If the love of the past predominates in the work, that is only because it predominates for Wilcher as well. And the balance between the opposed views—slightly off as it is—is the balance of the trilogy as a whole as well. All three of the major characters eventually assent to a spiritual sense of life though each has had substantial losses, and each of the three praises life at the moment of death. Measured by the standard of the middle class—the social view which largely but not completely controls Wilcher's attitudes—each of the characters ends in failure. Wilcher himself builds up the estate, but upon his death Tolbrook will be divided among three heirs. Sara has risen in social class at the beginning of her career when she, a farm girl, marries Matt Monday of the middle class. After marriage, she regresses socially at a steady rate into the lower levels of the urban proletariat. Gulley's social mobility is shown in his movement from the middle class of his father, an academy artist, to poverty and the bohemianism which is a twentieth-century exclusion from all social classes.

The second trilogy shows movement in social class in two directions with Nimmo's rising in class from his father's status as foreman farmer to his own position as wealthy politician and company director. At the same time, the Latters' inability to keep up with change makes them lose a good deal of their wealth and social position. In the same sense, Nina's marriage is the alignment of the falling upper-middle class, whose power was being reduced, with the rising lower class.

The general view concerning the historical development of the period from about 1880 to the 1940's covered in Cary's novels assumes that the immediately preceding Victorian age had been one of high tradition, that accepted life in heroic terms, and gave to its children the necessary sense of order and rules, serving the real needs of men and women. This period was followed by a transitional two decades, from about 1880 to about 1900, which reacted to the earlier Victorian years with an aesthetic decadence and which prepared the way for a fuller break with the past of the more political period before the First World War. This break was completed by the war and by the economic and industrial changes which accompanied social and intellectual change. The main effect of this period of change in Cary's books is seen in the lack of direction the period was able to give to its young, producing thus the dull generation of Tabitha's John and Bessie's Iris. The postwar twenties and thirties formed two decades in which the enthusiasm for science and the distrust of emotion were symptoms of a lack of acceptance of human nature. The children produced by this generation, however, accepted in the period of the Second World War and the years immediately following a new sense of responsibility, which was different from the heroism associated with the Victorian age, but which nevertheless again accepted life, creativity, and the family.

The formal development used in the books to show this process of history is begun by showing the past as a firm standard which becomes diffused and weakened by later periods. The later development also shows the standards of the past as being not nearly so firm as they first appear to be. The effect is somewhat similar to that of the earlier works which first show, say, the white group in *The African Witch* as a single unified entity, but which subsequently correct this view by showing the dissensions in the white community. At the same time the standard which seems to make the world of old John Corner a period of firmness with no fundamental divisions is seen to contain very real dissensions which exist in his household and among his tenants. Just as the earlier works show a social situation and then fill it in by showing the details of conflict, so the historical works show a temporal situation and then fill in the details, including the conflicts and divisions.

In both groups of works the fundamental interest is the same. All of Cary's works could well be described as an attempt to show the actual position of the individual, in context of all the forces which influence him and which he in turn affects. *Castle Corner* and *Mister Johnson,* books which are firmly opposed, both fit into this general pattern: *Castle Corner* has the widest scope in space, *Mister Johnson* has the narrowest; *Castle Corner* has the biggest cast of characters; *Mister Johnson* has the smallest; *Castle Corner* places major emphasis on the widespread sociological conditions, while the emphasis in *Mister Johnson* is on the individual affected by them. And *Castle Corner* stresses multiplicity of causes, while *Mister Johnson* stresses the unity of effect. In spite of such differences, however, the works clearly serve the same general function, as do the works in which the primary interest is historical. A major difference in approach, however, is that in the historical works the relationship is not between the sociological and the personal, but rather between the historical and the typical. Rather than showing, as *Castle Corner* and *Mister Johnson* both do in their different ways, how the individual is affected by the multiple forces operating on him, the historical works show the eternally human character constantly reappearing in changed historical conditions.

In *A Fearful Joy* and *The Moonlight* the constant theme

is the nature of woman. *The Moonlight* focuses more directly on the description of the nature of women; *A Fearful Joy* focuses more directly on the changing historical scene, but the books are two sides of the same coin. The two trilogies go much further, in the sense that they deal not only with three basic human types (conserver, nester, creator) but they deal also with the interrelatedness of the three. Thus in the trilogies there is an expansion in space as well as in time, in history working on the typically human as well as in sociology working on the uniquely individual.

These related contrasts in Cary's works can be seen as a development of the contrasts in Cary between the external and the internal, the objective and the subjective. *Castle Corner* with its emphasis on multiplicity is an attempt to define a moment in history by piling up the sum of its details; this explains its wide scope. *Mister Johnson* with its emphasis on the unique and the personal is an attempt to define the effect of history by showing its meaning for a single individual; this explains its narrow view. The trilogies are a major attempt to combine both views, while the early African works are content to leave the two views separated by an unbridgeable gap.

What is quite clear is that Cary insists on the simultaneous presence of both views in his reality, from his earliest published works through the latest. This insistence on duality is closely related to Cary's division between the objective fact and its inner significance, the division which allows Aissa to appear as objectively wrong and subjectively valuable. It can make Johnson socially a victim and personally a victor; it can make Gulley appear as a failure and success simultaneously, and can almost make believable the enormous split in the three major characters of the second trilogy.

The same division affects the concept of history in Cary's works. Seen in this way, the division becomes that between the single, unifying view of the hedgehog and the multiple view of the fox, in the metaphor of Isaiah Berlin's significant study of Tolstoy. As Berlin describes it, the fox views reality as "a collection of separate entities," while the hedgehog sees it as some "vast unitary whole." [10] When Cary's work is objectively adding detail to detail it is looking with the view of the fox; when it is subjectively describing one individual's way it is looking with the view of the hedgehog. Of more than casual interest is Berlin's point that Tolstoy used both views, since he "was by nature a fox, but believed in being a hedgehog." [11] Similarly, it is quite clear that Cary used both views, though he was apparently quite aware of his double vision, and indeed insisted on it.

Of more than marginal interest is another connection between Cary and Berlin's study of Tolstoy. While Cary continually shows the lack of reality in abstractions, Berlin repeatedly points to Tolstoy's distrust of the mystical and abstract.[12] In another parallel, Berlin emphasizes Tolstoy's similar distrust of the official version of events. For instance, Berlin speaks of the juxtaposition in *War and Peace* of " 'reality' —what 'really' occurred—with the distorting medium through which it will later be presented in official accounts offered to the public." [13] In Cary, similar juxtapositions form a basic principle of organization.[14]

With such a view of reality, Cary's typical technique must be basically one of elaboration and accretion. His books are, in effect, an accumulation of details to show the process of the "real," since at least one major part of reality is the total conglomeration of external details which make up any given situation. An event does not objectively have a single significant shape; it has an infinite number of details. Time does not flow, but is the medium within which a great many individual acts take place. This may well be the reason why all of Cary's books consist of short chapters, with hardly any single action smoothly developed in a single movement of storytelling. In the earlier books, the quickly shifting points of view show the multiplicity of forces, and prevent the long sweep of action. In the historical works, action is shown as fragmented in time. In the trilogies, the over-all construction controls three conflicting points of view. The action itself is broken, discontinuous, apparently frantic.[15]

The form of the books thus rejects the basis of much of

modern literature—that reality can be apprehended in a single sweeping form, pattern, or image. The form in Cary's books consists of continual interruptions, so as to show reality as a combination of details. The most obvious example is *Castle Corner,* where the events in Ireland, England, and Africa continually interrupt each other, often at critical moments of the plot. But the same kind of interruption comes in the opening of Cary's first published book when *Aissa Saved* begins with a description of the multisided situation of the Christians and then shifts to a description of the multisided situation of the pagans. The trilogy form itself can be seen as a natural development of Cary's aesthetic and intellectual needs. The trilogies show reality as a totality, an accretion of separate units, rather than as a panoramic sweep.

If the changing form of Cary's fiction shows a consistent unity, there is a major difference too. In the early books the sociological emphasis, the assumption of wide differences which individuals and groups make from within their own points of view, and the difference between the subjective and the objective meanings of acts make possible an insistent irony which is missing almost completely from the historical works and which is present in an entirely different way in the trilogies.

One bit of irony results from the necessary separation of people. Different backgrounds, and different views of the world, prevent one man from understanding the quality of another man's life. The irony is especially directed towards the British in Africa who make the mistake of thinking that they know the way of life in Africa, while in fact they have a very limited notion of what is really happening under their noses. Bradgate, for instance, the resident in *Aissa Saved,* is completely unaware that a woman trying to report a kidnapping is being gagged and tied in back of him at a public meeting (121 *AS*). Rudbeck is unaware of the extent of Johnson's money troubles, though the entire town is discussing them (68 *Mr J*). In *The African Witch* and in *Aissa Saved,* neither the missionaries nor the administration know anything of the parallel religious institutions the natives have in the vicinity of the missions themselves, where they develop their mixture of Christianity and native ju-ju. As *Aissa Saved* has it, "most missions . . . have private meeting places outside the official boundary. . . . It is in the mission club house . . . that Christian ideas are most eagerly discussed and the Bible searched for information and prophecies" (127 *AS*). In one of these meeting places the head of the murdered missionary, Schlemm, is put to use as a ju-ju object, thus serving as a metaphor of the religious confusion among the Africans. The missionaries are ignorant of the existence of these parallel missions and they are equally ignorant of the real meaning of Christianity for their converts. Part of the difficulty is one of language but the difference in the language represents a more basic cultural difference; an example is the Christian concept of repentance which is not really understood in Kolu, because the word which stands for it refers to the physical act of bowing to the ground as well as the idea of repentance. As a result, one of the natives can explain how he repented by pointing to a scar on his forehead as definite proof (41 *AS*).

Related to this is Aissa's understanding of communion as a literal eating of the body and blood of Christ (153–54 *AS*). Her notion of Christian love closely parallels physical love, and her notion of sacrifice is shown to be a businesslike arrangement between two parties. Ojo, similarly, has a literal belief in the effectiveness of prayer and does not quite accept Carr's explanations that, "It's not for us to know why God sends the rain or keeps it back" (130 *AS*), and that God grants prayers only "In His own time" (130 *AS*). Schlemm has a very similar discussion with Coker though it is a much more bitter one. When Schlemm denies the existence of witches, Coker calls the Bible to his support and Schlemm, in a hurry, is forced to say, "Never mind about the Bible, Mr. Coker" (133 *Af W*).

Two further points grow out of this irony resulting from cultural misunderstanding. One is that understanding is change. What happens in Cary's books when people understand each other is not that one grasps intellectually a concept which until then has been foreign to him. Rather the point is that there can be no understanding without change in the individual in the way that Aissa is changed by merging her two worlds (the Christian and the native) into a single new construct.[16] Fisk, in his significant grasp of Aladai's position, too, is changed as is Rudbeck when he finally makes human contact with Johnson.

Another point is that all developed human institutions have a basis in fundamental human patterns of thinking or feeling. Modern Christianity thus is an ethical development of religious acts originally closer to the basic human pattern. When Aissa thinks of sacrifice, for instance, as the actual giving of what means most to her, the sacrifice of her son, she is within the realm of meaning of the term sacrifice as used by the Carrs. She sees the term more basically, more physically; they see it more spiritually; the term itself includes both levels. Her view of communion as a literal eating of the God is implicit in the Carrs' notion of communion. Ojo's view of prayer as demanding immediate effectiveness is a basic view of Christian prayer.[17] Coker's call for blood comes from the same fundamental religious impulse which lies at the very roots of Christianity. The image which describes his theology suggests the connection with the original impulse: "the hot fountain shot out of primaeval mud" (50 *Af W*).

Misunderstandings in Africa occur not only in religious areas. In *An American Visitor* Gore and Cottee are able to think they are being greeted warmly when the natives are actually yelling, "Death to the whites" (79 *Am V*). Bewsher is involved in a misunderstanding which is very similar when he gives a long lecture to the assembled Birri chiefs on his views of federation, apparently unaware that they have federated in opposition to him, and that his arrival interrupted a discussion of how best to dispose of his body after he is murdered (165–67 *Am V*). The same misunderstanding leads to his death at the hand of his chief disciple, who commits the killing while shouting the nationalist cry taught to him by Bewsher (229 *Am V*).

In *The African Witch* Burwash appears unable to discuss

the question of a mosque and a ju-ju house, one of which has to be removed to make room for a road. Burwash's assumption is that anything old must be valuable to the natives. The native chief assumes that the building which is in better shape deserves retention. Aside from the irony of the reversal, in which the supposedly efficient European argues for reverence, and the supposedly religious native argues for efficiency, there is the irony of the inability of two people to understand each other's terms.

> "But the *ju-ju* house is new, lord," said the old ward chief.
>
> "So I say, and therefore it can be moved."
>
> "But the mosque is old, lord; it is the *ju-ju* house which is new."
>
> "Yes, yes, chief. I understand. And I say I wish to preserve your mosque, but in that case the *ju-ju* house will have to go."
>
> "Master, King of the World, it is the *ju-ju* house we must keep; it is new—the *ju-ju* house is the new building, just finished, only five years. It is the mosque which is—"
>
> "Yes, yes, chief," said the judge, and then, puzzled by the man's excitement, he turned to the crowd, and asked, "He means that the mosque is old, the *ju-ju* house new?" (82 *Af W*).[18]

The inability to make contact here is very similar to the lack of communication between Bamu and Johnson, whose difference is as much personal as it is sociological, and whose conversations show two people talking without any communication. When he is courting her and talks of love and beauty, she wants to know why he is so strange. When Johnson exclaims, "You are the most beautiful and the nicest girl in Fada," she asks her brother, Aliu, "From the South?" (28 *Mr J*). When he is fired by Rudbeck and she wants to leave him again, the conversation between them is of the same type:

> "Bamu, you don't want to go home?"
>
> "Yes, I'm going now."
>
> "But, Bamu, I'm just about to make you rich."
>
> "I don't want to be rich. I want to go home."

"But, Bamu, don't you 'gree for me?"

"No, I don't."

"Haven't I done work for you?"

"Yes."

"What then do you want?"

"You're mad."

"She means you're mad," Aliu explains (185 *Mr J*).

Of course the point is not whether Bamu is right or not, or whether her decision to leave is reasonable or not. The two are just unable to communicate.

Even people from the same group and with more or less the same upbringing cannot communicate at critical moments, as for instance, when two normally intelligent natives are panic-stricken at the assumption that the other is a witch (58 *Af W*).

While these books point out that men are bound together as well as divided, it is most curious that not only the division is seen ironically. The awareness that men share similarities under the cultural differences, comes also with an ironic force. For instance Johnson and the trader Gollup get drunk together and discuss their families and philosophies. They begin by similarly praising their wives, though it is obvious that both are creating descriptions of women which do not correspond to reality, they go on to discuss a similar acceptance of the white man's burden, and they end with similar sentimentality (127–31 *Mr J*). The effect of the passage is ironic partly because each is creating a reality for himself in which he is not really living, and while they seem to be speaking to each other they are really addressing themselves. More fundamentally the irony stems from the curious coincidence of views between these two men of different races, who live as master and servant, and whose relationship eventually becomes that of murderer and victim, largely because each cannot have a fully human relationship. The book contains a similar connection between Rudbeck and Johnson, and, more surprisingly, between Bamu and Rudbeck's wife Celia. Like Bamu, Celia is unable to see the reality shown to her because she thinks in predetermined patterns. Looking at Fada, "she does not see it at all. She does not see the truth of its real being, but the romance of her ideas . . ." (106 *Mr J*). Like Bamu she is unable to talk to her husband. When he is upset because the road is finished, she asks, like a mother amusing the children, "Couldn't you do one more little road?" And when Rudbeck continues the conversation, somewhat sarcastically, she changes to a topic equally significant to her, "Oh, dear, is that another hole in your shirt?" (166 *Mr J*).

A similar ironic effect comes from the description of social and religious patterns, which are totally foreign to the European tradition in terms which are acceptable to Europeans. For instance, the trial which finds Aissa guilty of witchcraft is conducted with principles of decency and justice which would be praised in England. Decorum is kept by "a public-spirited young woman" who hits Aissa in the mouth when she interferes with the dignity of the occasion (85 *AS*). The judge who finds her guilty is meticulous in his honesty and in his skillful evaluations of the truthfulness of the witnesses. The boy who brings the pestle which is used to break her ankles is "intelligent and enterprising beyond his years" (86 *AS*). In the same way, the ju-ju in *The African Witch* is seen as operating in rationalistic patterns. The irony in these cases is not simply one directed at the British who call the natives "trousered apes," while they are shown to be similar apes dressed in different trousers. The irony goes deeper and shows that the similarity of human responses is no less and no more a fact than the necessary misunderstandings and variations of human culture. This point is made in *An American Visitor* when social change causes both Marie's boy Henry and the English Cottee to react in the same way. Like Cottee, Henry urges change as an expression of freedom, and it makes little difference that the change Henry accepts includes incest (162–63 *Am V*). Like Cottee too, Henry makes money out of the unsettled conditions which follow the conflict between the natives and the whites. Again it makes little difference that Henry makes his money out of transactions which include condemned tinned meats, aphrodisiacs, smuggled gin, and abortions (233 *Am V*), or that Cottee is going to spend some of his wealth on the opera (236 *Am V*). The similarity between the two men can be evaluated according to Cottee's own standards, and Cottee says in a slightly different context that only the general principle matters, not its specific form (152 *Am V*).

Finally the most far-reaching aspect of the irony in these early works concerns the impossibility of organizing man's life rationally, in an orderly way, and the absence of any final justice. First of all, hardly any character in any of the books is really aware of what he is doing. Quite aside from the absence of planning among the British, or the absence of a general view among the natives, there is the difference between the subjectively created world in which each man lives and the objective world in which his actions have effect. Thus, for instance, both Burwash and the emir of *The African Witch* grossly overestimate their places and influences upon Rimi affairs. The emir still thinks of himself as the center of Rimi without whom nothing gets done, and only the technical question of settling definitely on his successor keeps him from the assassination which shortly follows (178–83 *Af W*). However, the full weight of the irony of *The African Witch* is implicit in the very structure of the work, which goes from Aladai's original invasion, full of the promise of progress, to the final invasion, which causes his useless death. His death, though clearly a defeat for him and for rationality, is however not shown as a triumph for any evil person or principle; it only shows what a muddle reality turns out to be. None of the characters in the book are evil, in the sense that any one freely chooses the bad when he is aware and is free to choose the good. Furthermore, the several who are seen as destructive, such as Honeywood in his mechanical stupidity, or Coker in his emotional geyser are not in themselves as strong or as capable as their more constructive counterparts. Most of the people involved have at least their share of good will, and this includes the fairly incompetent Burwash. The book seems to conclude by asking how is it possible under these circumstances for the events in Rimi to have brought about so much less progress than might have been possible? [19]

The answer to this question is seen more clearly in *Mister Johnson,* where the road becomes another case in point of a similar defeat of progress. Partly because the British fail to plan, and partly because freedom is by nature uncontrolled, the opening of the road is not a formal event, and its effects are not expected. Rather, the road opens itself (163 *Mr J*), bringing change and progress willy-nilly, along with the disorder which can be measured immediately by the increase in crime which follows it to Fada (207 *Mr J*). An even clearer case of the unexpected is that of Johnson himself, the result of the well-meaning civilizing force. Moreover, as has already been noted, the element in Johnson which leads him to his death is the same element which leads him to his triumph. This is seen for instance in his enforced stay as a penniless stray at the *zungo* which he himself built. The quality of imagination and daring which frees him from convention in order to create poetry and build a road is the same quality which leads him to rob and murder. In neither case does he act according to the moral which he expresses after seeing the Waziri's favorite in prison: "It makes you think that a chap has to look out for himself—yes, you've got to be careful" (202 *Mr J*). Throughout his life Johnson is no more able to "look out for himself" than Gulley Jimson is able to heed his own advice, "IT'S WISE TO BE WISE."

The real lesson is that life and change are sure to come, and that life on the whole means progress, but the irony is that, especially in individual cases, justice is only an accident. This point is a major one in *The Horse's Mouth* where Plant's Spinozist insistence on justice has a ridiculous conclusion, with Plant acting as king of a flophouse because he has the key to the bathroom. Gulley's Blakean ideal of freedom is more successful, not in any objective sense, but because it lets him subjectively recreate his world.

There is this fundamentally ironic view in all of Cary. And most of the novels have an additional level of irony in that they show the real—that is, subjective—truth of a character who is seen by society as a sinner. Aissa murders her child, Aladai is a nationalist revolutionary, Johnson is a murderer,

Charley is a juvenile delinquent, Sara is a convicted thief, Wilcher is an arsonist and exhibitionist, Wilcher winds up as a murderer as does Ella Venn, Tabitha is a demimondaine, Nina is an adulteress and gives false testimony, Nimmo is a crooked politician, Jim is a murderer and adulterer. By showing the difference in each case between the objective evaluation which society places on the facts which earn for each character his label, and the subjective quality which led each to his act almost inevitably, the books force us into an ironic double awareness.

The specifically historical works, beyond minor ironic touches call attention to the irony of a world which creates in men a desire for justice and order without permitting this desire to be satisfied. These books are nearly free of irony, perhaps because they contain so little emphasis on the isolated nature of experience. As a result, neither the lack of communication between individuals or groups, nor the unexpected parallels between them can strike with ironic force. In *Charley Is My Darling* as well, the irony is very limited, consisting almost entirely of the lack of communication between adults and children.

In the two trilogies, the irony is slightly different in form because it comes as a result of the interaction between the three separate narrators, but it is not really different in essence. First there is the ironic effect which comes from the exposure of the vanities and needs which make all of the characters omit the embarrassing events. It can be taken for granted that Nimmo for instance tells of the past (in part at least) because that is how he can avoid the events most difficult to justify. It is surely no oversight which makes Jim detail Nimmo's iniquities but makes him forget to stress with similar truthfulness his own adultery with Nimmo's wife, or which make Wilcher glide over his exhibitionism. Aside from the irony indicated in these examples there are two other kinds of irony. The first as in the earlier works suggests the lack of justice in life, for instance how little rearrangement of the history which actually did occur would be required to give Nina a happy life, and how much Gulley has given up for so little measurable reward. The second type of irony comes as a result of the implicitly stated inability to grasp reality except in the limited, subjective way made possible by the multiple vision of the work. It is this irony which finally suggests how little the individual understands of what he actually is doing, of the forces working on him, and of the effects he has on others. What Nimmo takes as a sign of grace indicating that he and Nina are closely united in spirit, Nina knows to be a sexual trick which she has learned from her lover. Nina sees the trick, Nimmo sees the spiritual result, Jim sees the lie.

## *Notes*

1 While Amanda is trying to reject the past here as undesirable, the context of the book makes it clear that the Victorian period accepted woman for what she was. Amanda's rejection of it is actually her attempt to reject her own femininity. For Cary's view that the Victorian period was true to the nature of woman, while the post-World War I period was an aberration which tried to deny her nature, see his articles "The Revolution of the Women," *Vogue*, CXVII (March 15, 1951), 99, 100, 149; and "Joyce Cary's Last Look at His Worlds," *Vogue*, CXXX (August 15, 1957), 150–51, 153.

2 Stanley Weintraub, "*Castle Corner*, Joyce Cary's *Buddenbrooks*," *Wisconsin Studies in Literature*, V (1964), 54–63, is an unconvincing attempt to connect Cary's *familienroman* with Mann's. Weintraub, incidentally, mentions that he is investigating "parody and parallel" in Cary of Tolstoy, Conrad, and Kipling.

3 Venn is only one of the long list of fathers who fail to have any real relationship with their children. Jim Latter's children are not brought up by him at all; Gulley believes it wrong to tamper with children; Charley's father appears once, shrewdly and briefly; Felix Corner thinks; John Chass enjoys himself; Bonser boasts; even the father in *A House of Children*, charming and capable as he is, appears only for occasional moments. The only exception is Chester Nimmo's father who had a very real effect on his children though he certainly does not pay a great deal of attention to them. Even the effect may be the result only of the special needs of Nimmo's book, which requires him to speak highly of family affection. Nimmo's own curious relationship to "his" children is the result largely of his own needs.

4 Whatever modern, psychologically oriented minds may think are the reasons for Rose's self-denial, the book itself suggests only moral strength as her motives.

5 The point is made repeatedly in the nonfiction. This is not to say, however, that all periods are equally praiseworthy. Some periods are greater than others because they allow the real needs of men to be more directly fulfilled. See the Prefaces to the Carfax editions of *Castle Corner, A Fearful Joy,* and *The Moonlight;* "The Idea of Progress," *Cornhill,* CLXVII (1954), 331–37; "The Front-Line Feeling," *The Listener,* XLVII (January 17, 1952), 92–93; "The Revolution of the Women"; and "Joyce Cary's Last Look at His Worlds."

6 In the Preface to the Carfax edition, Cary makes this point explicit by pointing out that Nancy "begins to create about herself those elements of order and responsibility that—in Tabitha's gloomy view—had disappeared from the world with the Victorians" (6–7 *FJ*). Characteristically he cut out passages which made this point too obvious in the book, passages which "seem to take him [the reader] by the lapel and say, 'Look here, just when everything seems to be in dissolution . . . see, a new world is being born'" (7 *FJ*). In cutting these passages Cary was following his standard technique of revision, which consisted in large part of cutting out explicitly stated ideas from his novels. Such excision, of course, does not in the least indicate that he did not want the reader to wind up with these ideas from other sources.

7 Cf. also Wilcher's masochism.

8 Gollan's de Havilland-like dedication to flying helps further to show his responsiveness to the new. That it nearly ruins him is another example in Cary of the self-destructiveness inherent in the imaginative man. A third element of the attack on Victorianism took political form, according to the book, but although it is mentioned—"It's politics or nothing," says Manklow, the editor who accurately judges public taste (98 *FJ*)—Tabitha has no connection with it.

9 An interesting similarity to the marriage between Bill and Amy is that between Catto and Francie Bill, a girl who like Amy is used by the family, in the short story, "A Good Investment." He marries her originally because of his practical nature, but then falls in love with her. The coincidence of Francie's last name with Bill's is matched by the similarity between Catto and Hatto, the name of the practical romantic in *Castle Corner.* The story is in *Spring Song,* pp. 62–78.

10 Isaiah Berlin, *The Hedgehog and The Fox* (New York: Simon and Schuster, 1953), p. 39.

11 *Ibid.,* p. 4.

12 *Ibid.,* p. 10, and *passim.*

13 *Ibid.,* p. 15.

14 Cf. Chapter Three, above, "The Official and the Personal." The relation suggested here is not so much between Cary and Tolstoy, though Tolstoy was much admired and much discussed by Cary, but between Cary and Berlin's discussion of historical truth.

In response to my questions about Cary, Berlin states that he does not believe their relationship to be more than coincidental. "Indeed I knew Cary," Sir Isaiah writes in a letter, February 7, 1966, "but I do not suppose that he read my writings, and I did not read his novels. I used to talk to him—about Tolstoy among other subjects—but I never expounded my ideas to him. He may have spoken about his to me—but I do not recollect any specific occasion, or any specific discussion. I do not believe that there is any direct connection between his ideas and mine . . . it may be that we were in natural sympathy. I used to find his company interesting and delightful—he was a wonderful story-teller—but we were not intimate friends; scarcely friends at all but acquaintances bound by much mutual good feeling. If there is any coincidence between our ideas, this must be attributed to coincidence or the Zeitgeist."

15 Cf. Cary's remarks on time in *Power in Men*. There is no such thing as the passage of time, he says there. It "does not pass; it adds to itself." In a comment which has bearing on Cary's descriptions of man as objective fact, he denies the notion that the present does not exist, and that man thus has no permanent self. "But man's self, of course, has the same kind, though not the same degree, of permanency as the character of any element, iron or oxygen, does." *Power in Men,* pp. 85–86.

16 Cf. Cary's description of the teacher who by making students "share his sympathetic reactions . . . changed them into different persons." *Art and Reality*, p. 68. See also *Power in Men*, p. 213.

17 Bloom says that *Aissa Saved* deals with religion only as psychological fact, and never tries to consider "whether religious formulations correspond with anything real." *Indeterminate World*, p. 48. Apparently Bloom requires dogmatic religious statements to satisfy his interest. Cary, on the other hand, believed that there is no division between psychological and external validity of religion. On the contrary, the real existence of religious facts is in man's mind, eternally recurring. Cf. also Hoffman's point that Cary is showing the roots of Christianity in primitive religion. *Joyce Cary*, p. 11.

18 Later the suggestion is made that his ignorance may be by design. He is concerned about the reaction of one of his superiors, Lepper, who apparently is especially concerned about the preservation of local antiquities (186 *Af W*).

19 It would be going a little too far to say with Mahood, pp. 191–92, that the book ends with *complete* hopelessness. In a minor conversation at Judy Coote's sickbed Rubin voices one of Cary's own opinions, that the world is moving towards greater security and democracy (302 *Af W*). The sergeant who reads so comically is also a sign of progress in spite of the ironic implications.

# 5. The Beliefs
and the Values

The body of Cary's beliefs is expressed in his novels, and, perhaps because the publication of his work was delayed so long, until as he said he had worked out his fundamental ideas,[1] they show a general consistency and cohesion. His interests seem to lie in history, philosophy, politics, religion—in fact, in the traditional areas of a liberal education. And he approaches these issues in the general commonsensical way of the nonspecialist, evading specialized terminology and always relating the abstractions to personal experience.

The fact is that Cary's interests in these matters are secondary. He has only one major concern—the actual position of the individual in the many-sided reality in which he lives. History, politics, philosophy—these are of course all part of the general obligation of an educated man. In addition, to find the influences on the individual, history is helpful; to find out what is "real"—basic in man—philosophy is helpful; religion is one of the most important edifices of man and thus indicates some of his basic modes of expressing himself, a clue to what he is.

Nor is Cary satisfied only with establishing what the position of man is. He is pragmatically concerned with values—what is the best kind of life, and with morality—how a man ought to live. His aesthetics have a similar pragmatism, being closely concerned with describing the actual process of creativity, as well as with establishing a system of values for art.

As a result, all his thinking is of a piece, the aesthetics running into history, the history running into religion, the religion running into the symbol, the symbol into the nature of reality. What lies under them all is Cary's epistemology, his assumption with the idealist philosophers that each man is forced by the nature of his being to build up his own version of reality; it is primarily in the quality of this construction and in his devotion to it that his fulfillment—his value as a human being—lies. Society is measured by the opportunities it provides for its members to construct their reality. Art is measured by its grasp of the reality, that is, by the artist's personal construction of his reality and by his ability through the symbol to reach into the privately created world of his readers.

The measure of every discussion, of every question, for Cary is its relation to the individual and its effect on him. This is what Cary means by "real," a word he uses to evaluate ideas or approaches. In identifying his basic bias at the beginning of *The Case for African Freedom,* for instance, he says, "In any political question, I ask first, how does this affect the real men on the ground, the people in their private lives?" [2] Political errors arise from ignoring this "real." "The greatest political mistakes, both in practice and in theory, have arisen from abstraction" is the opening sentence of a chapter called "Political Reality," and he goes on to explain what he means by the words: "In real history, if not in written history, the real overcomes the abstract; that is, the feelings and needs of human nature gradually shape politics and destroy or transform artificial divisions and abstract political constructions." [3] Hegel's view of history is in error because of a parallel mistake: Hegel does not take into account a physical reality which affects the needs and feelings of men; he failed "to establish a reality over against mind." [4] Marxist theory is wrong because it only accounts for a small part of what motivates men: "In leaving out of account the political and social factors, the ideal and religious movements, in isolating the economic process, it missed the truth and became useless or dangerous even to the communist revolution." [5] In the same way, beauty in a work of art means a proper relationship to the real. In *Art and Reality*, Cary phrases it this way:

> . . . when we recognize beauty in any ordered form of art, we are actually discovering new formal relations in a reality which is permanent and objective to ourselves. . . .[6]

In an earlier essay, he uses a more homey image, comparing the "right and significant form of any work of art" to ladies' fashions and pointing out that,

> . . . in the most beautiful form of dress, however different—the Moorish, the Indian, the different peasant costumes of Europe, the eighteenth century panniers, the Regency muslins, the crinolines, even the bustles—each has some relation to woman's nature, not only her physical nature but, by implication, the whole range of her special activity, her special powers as a woman.[7]

Cary's own system is rooted in what he believes to be the fundamental fact of man's existence, his necessary isolation. It is this isolation which makes it necessary for every human being to create the world for himself as an imaginative act. In *Power in Men*, published in 1939, Cary says that each child is "a free and distinct person, who cannot be deprived of his own private idea of the world. The child will form such an idea in any case, for it is a creative centre, and none or nothing can enter into his mind and create for it." [8] In 1956 Cary said, "Everyone . . . is presented with the same chaos [in actual life], and is obliged to form his own idea of the world, of what matters and what doesn't matter." [9] The word *obliged* here has the full force of necessity. Cary is not saying that man may form an idea of reality if he likes, but that he has no choice but to do so. "We are compelled, each of us, to form our own ideas of things," he says a few pages later. This isolated condition of man is the cause of man's freedom in the universe. "Without the gap between body and mind the individual would not exist," Cary argues. "He would be merely a part of universal nature, controlled completely by instinct, with all the limitations of creatures who are so controlled. It is the independent reason of man in which his individuality, his freedom, resides." [10] Man's isolated condition also makes man's most important attribute his imagination, or to add the adjective with which Cary ordinarily qualifies it, his "creative" imagination. For man's awareness of reality comes to him not through his intellect—even though Cary speaks of "independent reason" in the passage just quoted—but rather through his intuition. "The individual mind appears to itself as cut off from the general real except insofar as it can *intuit* that real," Cary says. [11]

Though man knows reality only through his own re-creation of it, and as a result every man's reality is uniquely his own, unlike that of anyone else, Cary takes it for granted that an objective reality does exist. [12] This reality, the permanent character of the world, consists of "permanent and highly obstinate facts, and permanent and highly obstinate human nature." [13] As usual, here Cary joins two seemingly opposed elements, while at the same time keeping them separate—at least verbally. This is his usual procedure and similarly he asserts the unity of the individual with the reality to which he seems to be opposed, of the spiritual element with the body, of the subject with the object. Even the title of Cary's book on aesthetics, *Art and Reality,* is meant to suggest the relationship between the two apparently opposed words. [14] In the novels this way of thinking may well explain why Cary was repeatedly concerned to show the division among men and social groups, while at the same time he insisted that these men and these groups together make up the one total situation, or why later on he chose to make it appear that he was opposing the fundamentally united characters of the trilogies. This tendency, related to the various technical devices which allow Cary to show the multiple elements of his total vision by accretion, can be seen also in Cary's predeliction for concepts of totality. In discussing the needs of Africa he asks where one ought to start in Africa, and answers, "everywhere at once." [15] The development he calls for is "total development." [16] Children, he insists, are formed by their "total experience." [17]

The personally-created version of reality must be at least minimally in proper relationship with objective reality if the individual is to survive. An example of dangerously overlooking "facts" occurs in the case of the boy who thought he could fly and jumped off the roof.[18] An example of a kind of reality which misgauges "human nature" is Hitler's, ". . . the kind of dream which fills the asylums with emperors and gods, men who have created for themselves impossible worlds." [19] The "facts" refer simply to the nonhuman world, the nature of rocks, the attraction of gravity, the qualities of hydrogen gas. "Human nature," not so simply, refers to fundamental human patterns, ways of thinking (though not ideas themselves), love, appetites. In denying that he is an existentialist in Sartre's sense of the word, apparently because he objects to Sartre's atheism, Cary says that, "I am influenced by the solitude of men's minds, but equally by the unity of their fundamental character and feelings, their sympathies which bring them together. I believe that there is such a thing as unselfish love and beauty." [20]

These fundamentals, whether they were developed before the fact or afterwards, support all of Cary's dogmatic views. There is an objective reality. Man can only know it through a personally constructed view. Therefore man is forced to be free, united to his fellow men by a common human nature consisting of his nonintellectual elements, and his imagination is his most fundamental characteristic. The philosophy is as clear as such philosophies ordinarily get, rather unexceptional, and fairly simple.

While these ideas are the basic ones, Cary's most important specific concept is his version of freedom, a concept which serves him as a standard for evaluating men and societies. For instance his idea of what human society ought to be like is contained primarily in *Power in Men,* a work somewhere between sociology and politics. His definition depends on the assumption that freedom is the most important human good, and that society ought to be organized so as to offer men that good most effectively. He begins by defining liberty and freedom as both positive and "real." Liberty, he says, is that which gives men power to control their lives, to make decisions. Freedom is the ability of men to make decisions. The society provides liberty insofar as it enables men to realize their native powers.[21] The norm which the society can use as a general goal is expressed in the phrase, "the greatest liberty, or free power, of the greatest number," [22] while the specific measure of liberty would be an index, similar to the cost of living index, which would include weighted figures for such disparate items as the income, the hours of leisure, the degree of education, the degree of political liberty.[23]

In *The Case for African Freedom* he makes it clear that political liberty, though "It is the crown and indispensable guardian of real freedom . . . comes at the end, instead of at the beginning, of a people's freedom." [24]

Cary spends a great portion of his discussion of liberty showing the inadequacy of the usual tendency to define it as the absence of restraint.[25] Such a negative definition, he thinks, is confusing because it makes all interference wrong, "So that it is a crime against liberty to arrest a pickpocket or to prevent a ship-owner from sending out his men in a rotten ship to get insurance money." [26] More to the immediate point, this definition of liberty also led to the policy of indirect rule for Africa which prevented the necessary development of the continent. It stressed the negative, the lack of interference, rather than the positive, the necessary advancement of Africans in education and economic power. However, it is only with adequate education and with an adequate standard of living that man can realize his own powers, and they are thus prerequisites to liberty. In spite of the injustice that is always a part of reality, "it is still the duty of government and parents to battle with luck, to try to give the equal chance. And the front line of that battle is education." [27]

The double dangers to liberty are the twin errors of anarchism and absolutism. Democracy, on the other hand, is not only the proper system of government, but also the inevitable one. This is the point of *The Process of Real Freedom*,[28] a product of the Second World War, and it is made often in his writings. In *Power in Men,* for instance, Cary says,

Democracy, therefore, like liberty, of which it is made, is real and indestructible. As liberty is the creative power of man, indivisible and unique, so democracy is power in many men combining together in society, according to its forms, and tending always, by the increase of that individual power, towards political authority. A democratic government is rulership in the people. It is natural government, as liberty is natural power.[29]

In the same way, Cary repeatedly insists that the world is moving in the direction of greater liberty. On the one hand, he insists that a world government, by which he means a world democracy, is coming: "World government is already in sight, although probably at a considerable distance. What the distance is nobody knows, or what the difficulties, perhaps the wars, by the way. But it is certainly coming." [30] On the other hand he insists that the modern world offers more liberty than previous eras. The opening sentence of one of his articles asks, "Is there such a thing as progress in the world?" and the answer is yes.[31] In the modern world there is greater demand for security and peace, there is more education, and there is more prosperity. In what *Vogue* magazine called his last look at his world, Cary said, "I so much prefer the modern world to the one I was born into." [32] In contrast, the apparent stability of the period before the First World War was based on an enormous mass of poverty and ignorance, Cary argues another time. And he summarizes his attitude towards that period: "People talk about the wonderful time before the Kaiser war—the good old days of peace and security. But the truth is of course that that security was bogus. It rested on a chance balance of powers." [33]

According to Cary the historical period with which he is concerned in his work, that is the period from the end of the nineteenth century to the post-Second World War years, shows a progess into liberty. The security of the pre-First World War period was a false one. Insofar as it examined itself at all it falsely assumed that the liberal world could face every crisis. The war destroyed this rationalism and brought in a period of confusion which was basically defeatist. Today people are not happier but they have more choices to make and are more aware of what they are doing. This view of history is at the basis of Cary's historical works.[34]

Parallel to this view is the notion of progress which is implicit in the African books, where the forces of modern civilization are all cooperating, often without knowing it, to bring greater liberty to the Africans. The Europeans constantly make mistakes and on the whole, even though their limitations are part of the total sociological situation, they do not meet their full responsibility. Nevertheless, the full effect of the European influence in Africa is in the long run desirable. The trashy white clothing which Akande Tom so covets in *The African Witch* is a flag of freedom and power to him and it is one of the things that leads him almost out of the ju-ju life into an educated life. If he returns to the ju-ju, that is a sign of the comparative failure of the administration led by such as Burwash. The progress is nonetheless there, and it is real, because whatever the faults of the European administration, the European presence gives the Africans a view of a desirable alternative to their own narrow lives. "Life in a primitive tribe is monotonous and boring," Cary says in a discussion of *Aissa Saved*. "It survives, when it does survive, only because the people who suffer it have no idea of anything better." [35] In *The Case for African Freedom*, he says similarly,

> But the ideal state, that which gives to all its members the best chance of happiness and realization, and makes the best use of their different powers, is obviously that with the greatest variety of social and economic organization. It is not the tribe with its single pattern of existence into which all must fit. . . .[36]

Akande Tom is not a tribal native, but his case illustrates Cary's point. He lives in a narrow world, directed by a single narrow track of social organization, and he is kept there by his ignorance, his lack of power to make an alternative choice, and by the lack of choices available to him in his society.

And yet, in Cary's books, characters demonstrate a widespread desire to keep the Africans in their tribal life. Some want this because they are racists and Cary thinks their argument so weak that it is not worth countering in detail. "We need not argue with the racialist," Cary says.[37] Others want this because they believe either in anarchy or in absolutism. The two apparently opposed political beliefs are closely related for Cary, who even drew up a kind of chart to explain the relationship:

Thus pure anarchist theory leads to absolutism; and absolutism always leads to anarchy. The double action can be shown thus:

Absolute individual right derived from nature or supreme God — implies — a nature or supreme God with absolute rights over all individuals,

and produces the absolute state or church, organized egotism.

Supreme nature or supreme God. Ideal or material dialectic.

Any automatic historical process. The infallible Bible. Volksgeist. The British spirit. Germania, Italia, Britannia, Hibernia, etc. — implies — individual right grounded in nature's or God's will for the individual. A fixed economic or historical function to which an individual has absolute right. Direct access to God's will and therefore absolute authority in him. Right in all who share the spirit to say, "I act in the name of the Volksgeist, etc., and no one can gainsay my right,"

and leads to anarchy, disorganized egotism.[38]

The mistake of the anarchists is their assumption that there is one fixed natural system of society, that men left alone will somehow choose it, that men are not naturally pugnacious, and that primitive states in general have no formal system to assure compliance with social patterns. Such is the belief of Mary Hasluck in *An American Visitor* before she learns better, but it is also the rationale of all those who prefer the naked warrior to the "trousered ape," as well as the rationale of all the characters in the novels who refuse to teach children because they are afraid education will somehow spoil them. Into this category fit Pinto, of *A House of Children*, Lommax, the artist in *Charley Is My Darling*, as well as Gulley Jimson.

The root of the absolutist is the belief that the individual man is helpless before the injustice of life and history.[39] This category includes at least one side of Cottee in *An American Visitor* and old John Corner. But the relationship between the two points of view is a main organizing principle of the first trilogy, where Gulley is the thoroughgoing anarchist, Wilcher is divided between his absolutist temperament and his anarchistic hopes, and where a large collection of London anarchist-absolutists surround Plant with a mixture of Spinozist, Rousseauvian, Marxist, and Ruskinian philosophies. The same relationship organizes *The Moonlight*, where Rose and Ella Venn represent two not very distant poles; the second trilogy, where Chester Nimmo and Jim Latter illustrate clearly how easy it is especially for the convinced man to move from one camp into the other with hardly a ripple of awareness; and *The Captive and the Free*, where Preedy walks the tightrope that separates the two views. Of Cary's last nine novels, if the posthumous *The Captive and the Free* can be included, eight deal in a fundamental way with the anarchism-absolutism relationship, and the theme comes visibly to the surface in just about all of them.

Important as the theme is in the novels, the relationship between absolutism and anarchism, like the whole question of liberty with which it is connected—the whole question of the political way of looking at freedom—is not the most fundamental issue. It is a theme, it is a context, it affects individuals, it serves even as a standard of evaluating characters and historical events. But what Cary says of his index of liberty applies here too:

It can grade the liberties of the people only by their economic power, their hours of work and leisure, their standards of education, their votes, and their freedom to know.

The character of reality itself, its final being, is not to be measured.[40]

The final evaluation, the character of reality, lies not in the question of liberty, but rather in the question of freedom.

The major distinguishing characteristic of Cary's thinking in his nonfictional prose as well as in his fiction is his insistence on the freedom of the individual. To state exactly what this freedom is, however, requires some close examination. Given Cary's definition of liberty as a positive power, it follows that, as he says in *The Case for African Freedom,* "Real freedom . . . can be greatly increased by social organization." [41] But besides separating freedom from liberty, Cary also sees freedom in the individual to be of several kinds. In *Power in Men,* for instance, he distinguishes between what he calls "moral freedom" and what he calls "freedom of the mind." Using the cases of Socrates and Galileo as examples, he explains that the judges in both cases had moral freedom. Galileo and Socrates, however, also had freedom of the mind; that is, they tried to know the truth and to form their judgments upon facts.[42] Everyone, he says repeatedly, has moral freedom and everyone has the same moral values. But freedom of the mind varies with the man; it is the ability to accept new truth. Another time he speaks of freedom as the ability to create something new: "Have men liberty to form their own purposes and so to do what they like? Can they create and invent, or are they automatic machines? Did Dante, Shakespeare, Milton, Goethe originate anything, or were they barrel-organs?" [43] Still another time he speaks of freedom as, "in the strictest sense of the words, the life of the spirit; eternal life; the power of the individual soul." [44]

Although Cary's acceptance of freedom as a good in itself is implicit in everything he writes, he yet makes a point of saying that freedom in itself is not a value. "But freedom and liberty by themselves are not values. They are only the ground of value. A man can have a mind free from prejudice, and liberty of action, and choose to act badly. We do not say that all free-minded men are good or that all good men are free-minded." [45] Moral standards are not useful as a standard of value either, Cary makes a point of saying: "All people admire courage, generosity, unselfish devotion. But moral approval has been given to the nazi revolution as well as the Spanish. It has been used to justify the shooting of communists in Spain as well as kulaks in Russia." [46] Earlier in this book he has also praised the judges of Galileo as good men.[47]

One positive value that Cary does accept as standard is the degree of sincerity in a man's character, and the sincerity evidences itself by the risk he takes for his belief, that is, by the degree of his selflessness. Speaking of how to test the quality of a man's political beliefs, Cary says that if he is sincere, "He will risk something, his skin or his job, to bring in that form of society which satisfies his moral will. This test in real life will divide the true men from the parasites." [48] He praises art, incidentally for a very similar quality. The enjoyment of the simplest form of art makes life valuable, he says in *Art and Reality*, because "that enjoyment has no relation with appetite or self-satisfaction. It is something freely given, a good, a grace, belonging simply to existence, to reality itself." [49]

The clue to Cary's high valuation of freedom lies here. Freedom is valuable because it brings man in tune with reality itself. If he is not free he is a machine, and as such not alive, not in tune with reality. It is by his freedom that man loves and creates, and to deny that freedom is to deny his own life. "To say to a man 'You shall not love' is to say 'You shall not live like a man, but like a machine.' It is either useless or it destroys the man as a man." [50]

Having asserted all this about freedom it remains for Cary to show that freedom is in fact possible for man, that his being is not determined by a chain of events in his life, which work on him according to fixed laws. This is what he tried to do specifically in a note appended to *Power in Men*. He begins by rejecting the use of the common term, *free will,* for the discussion. If a man has a will, it is a purpose and purpose cannot be free, Cary argues, apparently to forestall the argument that every action fulfills a desire and is to that extent determined. Cary pushes the question one step further back and asks whether man has the power to determine his purposes. The example he uses is that of a man giving sixpence to a beggar. The giving, he says, is not free; the man gives because he wants to. Once that has been determined the giving is no more free "than a tool in his hand is free." But the question then becomes, why does the man want to give the sixpence, or as Cary phrases it, "Have men liberty to form their own purposes and so to do what they like?" [51]

Of course, Cary's answer is yes. But strangely enough, it is not an unhesitating affirmative. Rather, he approaches the question first by means of an analogy which, as he realizes himself, is not quite appropriate. History, according to the analogy,

> . . . is like a tapestry made of coloured threads. Each thread is a continuous chain of determined events, of atomic movement. It is absolutely unbroken and eternal. It goes on for ever, in this world or another. But the creative mind weaves the threads into patterns which are always new and are never repeated. If the threads broke, the mind could not work; but without the mind to weave the pattern, they would have no history.[52]

Cary is aware of the fault in the analogy—that it falsely assumes man to stand outside of the tapestry and so outside of history itself—but he does not attempt to resolve the fault. Rather he simply asserts that freedom exists, along with determinism: "Life doesn't exist without matter or mind without body. Liberty cannot exist without determinism or determinism without liberty." [53] He concludes by saying that "we know that we have liberty exactly as we know that we are ourselves." [54] This can be taken to mean that it doesn't matter whether we are really free or not; if we exist we must accept the illusion which we have that we are free; or it may be taken to be a redundancy: *cogito ergo sum liber.* In either case logic is given up in favor of assertion.

Cary's freedom, then, is a concept based on his epistemology and his metaphysics and it has several dimensions.
There is an objective, external form of it, belonging essentially to society, and a subjective, internal, personal form of the
word, which includes moral freedom, freedom of the mind to
face new truth, and the creative life of the spirit.

Of course all of Cary's fiction is based on the views
which find dogmatic expression in his nonfiction, sometimes
very directly, sometimes less so. Cary said frequently that
his purpose was not to present ideas in his novels; indeed he
considers an author's intrusion into the novel to present his
own views as necessarily vain; it will not work.[55] But here he
is talking only of preaching and propagandizing. The last
thing in the world Cary would accept would be the thesis that
a novel could be written without a coherent view of reality.
One of the bases of *Art and Reality* is to disprove such an
assertion and, to cite only one clear statement from many,
Cary says there that "without some unifying idea, it is impossible for a book to have a form." [56] It is of course more than
clear in Cary's statement that the books he wrote in Africa
suffered from a lack of grounding in a view of the world, and
that he spent the ten years or so from the time he left the
African Service to the time he wrote *Aissa Saved* learning the
answers to fundamental questions about the nature of reality.[57] The lack of commitment which the books seem to indicate at first reading is only superficial. The objectivity is one
of technique. A closer examination shows the novels not only
to support Cary's expressed beliefs, but also to refine them and
show them in the greater actuality which fiction makes possible.

For the most part Cary's first three novels are shaped
around the difference between liberty and freedom, a difference which is both an effect and a cause of the interesting
formal device, the dual view which looks both from the outside and the inside, the objective and the subjective. The
ending of *An American Visitor,* for instance, alternating between Cottee's view of acceptance of a heroic world and the
realization that Bewsher and Marie are very wrong is soundly

based on the fact that while the two have lived free lives, their view will not develop liberty. In the same sense, *The African Witch* deals primarily with the problem of how to bring liberty to Africa, and loses the sense of vitality which the other African books have because it does not focus as directly on the issue of personal freedom. Aissa's death, also, is a failure in liberty, but it is a triumph of freedom.

M. M. Mahood, in her fine investigation of the African books, believes that the fundamental theme of these three books is "the distinction between self-reliance and self-abandonment." [58] She states her case very convincingly, by quoting Cary as saying that in *Aissa Saved,* "Carr's conversion in the second chapter and Ojo's and Aissa's discovery in the last that to be happy it is only necessary to abandon personal responsibility and give up all to Christ, are critical points. These are in fact surrenders—escapes of human nature overpowered by the responsibility of judgement, of choosing, into the bosom of a nurse." [59] Similarly in *The African Witch* Aladai and Rackham both surrender to the temptation of irresponsibility, along with Osi, Coker, and Dryas. Marie Hasluck's great error is also one of a willful release from the responsibility which human life requires. Yet, at least in *Aissa Saved,* Mahood is forced to question the scheme she has set up. Although according to her very convincing explanation, Cary's theme is to show the surrender of responsibility as failure and the assumption of responsibility as the only proper response to the conditions of life, Mrs. Carr and Aissa come out of the book as the most interesting, the most complex and, one might say, the most valued characters. She answers the point by explaining that Cary changed his intentions in the three years he took to write *Aissa Saved.* "During this time," Mahood explains, "his interest shifted from ethics and Ali to enthusiasm and Aissa. That is to say, he came increasingly to feel that life demanded a faith and not a code, the spirit rather than the letter." [60]

The question resolves itself more fundamentally with the realization that Cary distinguishes between the three kinds of freedoms, and that of the three he prizes most highly the creative life of the spirit, partly because it is the basis, it encompasses the others. This is the link which binds Aissa to Chester Nimmo and connects the first of his books to the last. In *Aissa Saved,* according to this view, Ali is free in the sense that he has freedom of the mind. More than Aissa, more than anyone else in the book, he is able to break out of the traditional ways of thinking and adopt a new code of justice and behavior. It is Aissa, however, who is more significantly free. The actual way in which her freedom expresses itself is a somewhat unusual one and it is one which Cary never fully explains outside of his fiction. Nevertheless this definition remains the standard of ultimate, subjective freedom through all of the fiction. She is free because she breaks completely from the bonds of what is ordinarily called selfishness and brings her life fully into accord with her own intuition of it. That is, she accedes to her own personality as fully as is possible.

She is far from free in the sense that she is responsible for the situation in which she finds herself. First of all, there is nothing to suggest that she is a self-made woman. Rather she is seen primarily as a product of external forces; her religious values are a result on the one hand of the large social, cultural, and political forces which control the relationship between the Europeans and the Africans; on the other hand she would not have developed her intense devotion or her confusion of religions if not for the accidental presence of the Carrs with their precise individual characteristics. Similarly, her predicament in town is the result of a chain of events which the book describes—the drought, Ojo's tenacious and selfless insistence on converting the pagans, Bradgate's ignorance of events, the reaction of the pagan priests, and the ineffectiveness of the native administration. Her personal characteristics are nowhere shown as freely chosen by her. Her extraordinary love for her child, her excesses of enjoyment and of dejection, for instance, are reactions apparently developed by events and forces over which she has no control.

Paradoxically, what makes her seem of special value is her inability to fool herself into being selfish. Her argument with Jesus at the end of the book, clearly describes the degree to which she is conscious of her own position among her multiple and at the moment contradictory desires. She loves her own life, she loves her husband Gajere, and most of all she loves her child. On the other hand, her devotion to Christianity means so much to her that she must sacrifice all that she loves most. She tries to protect her great loves, one by one, against the demands of her need to sacrifice, by fooling Jesus—that is, by fooling herself. But, and this is the important point, she will not let herself be fooled.

> But the spirit being inside Aissa, wrapped into every part of her being, knew her better than herself. It knew the wifely appetites of her body, the tingling love in her hands, the mother's desire of her full breasts, the greedy cunning of all her muscles, the deceit of her quick tongue and grimacing features, the pride, the vainglory of her obstinate heart, much sooner than her brain conceived a thought (202 *AS*).[61]

Aissa is not even free to make her most significant decision, or at least she is not free in the sense of feeling the decision as a free one. Rather she is driven by something inside of her, something which does not allow her ever to give less of herself than everything.

It is impossible, then, to stop at any precise moment during the interaction of Aissa's self and her external circumstances to say where she could have consciously changed her life in an intelligent way so as to save her life and her child's. To the suggestion that to a limited extent her life has come to this stage as a result of her own decisions, furthermore, one would have to say that each decision came about in the same way as this one. The question of her conscious responsibility therefore simply cannot be resolved at all. In this sense, her freedom cannot be evaluated. On the other hand, it is clear that her decision is her own, a personal one, whether she was ever free to change it or not. She made it because she could not do otherwise than follow her nature. In terms of Cary's epistemology, she acted in thorough dedication to her intuition of reality. Her value as a human being, like the value of all the characters which the novels seem to admire, comes from this accession to her own nature, which ultimately is also an accession to the reality of the world. Her freedom, then, cannot be evaluated, in the usual sense, by its practical effects. It is an ultimate, necessary good, without which no personal life can have meaning. If she could have had greater freedom of the mind, and greater liberty, her life would have been a better one, to be sure. But the standard which evaluates the freedom of her mind or her liberty—a practical standard which measures her control over the environment—does not exist on the same plane with that which evaluates her as a free person. Freedom comes first; it is the commitment to oneself and, insofar as it is knowable, to reality.

In this sense there is no difference between Aissa's freedom and that of Johnson. His freedom includes a greater freedom of the mind, but it is in its nature so nonintellectual that his legs have as much control over his total attitude as his mind. Similarly, Johnson's creativity in dealing with his environment comes from his feelings as much as his mind; it is his sympathy, self-created as it is, for Rudbeck which allows him to reach the inspiration of the bribery, the games, the poetry, and the other devices which allow the road to be built. His fate, too, is never decided consciously. Like Aissa he is a product of forces over which he has no control, sociological forces which are outside of his control completely, like the accidents which send Tring to the scene at just the wrong moment, and even the very background which has made him what he is. He is obviously responsible for what happens to himself but only in the sense that what he is leads to what he does. It is impossible in the context of the book to say clearly that he ever at any single point was able to change the course of events. Like Aissa, again, he is a valuable person because he accedes so completely to what he is, to his own nature, and thus to reality.

He provides a clear example of a kind of person who lacks moral direction in this ultimate kind of freedom. He is equally creative when he disdains the Waziri's suggestion that he steal government documents, when he creates a Bamu who exists nowhere but in his own imagination, when he creates the poetry which becomes the property of everyone who hears it, when he motivates the village chief to send his young men out to the road work, when he forms a nearly meaningful relationship to Gollup, and when he throws the last party which leads hardly without a break to the murder of Gollup and his own death. Freedom is the essence of life but in itself, as Cary has explicitly said, it is neither morally good nor morally bad. Of course Johnson has a moral sense, and of course another kind of life would have been more productive and more constructive. Also he makes mistakes, and eventually his mistaken view of Bamu leads him to a knock on the head which brings him to the gallows. Nevertheless his creativity is subjectively the same in each case, and in each case it is totally free; his freedom is totally unattached to gain, it is completely without selfishness, and thus it is in tune with the real, a good which cannot be evaluated.

Cary's high valuation of this kind of freedom in itself indicates that he does not place a very high value on the intellectual process. Indeed, he does not believe that intellect plays a great part in decision making. In general his characters do not typically make decisions in the way ordinarily shown in fiction, by weighing alternatives and choosing between them. A comment by Gore in *An American Visitor* indicates the nonintellectual motivation of men in general: "Nothing could be done for these people. It wasn't that they were too stupid to understand the position but that they didn't want to. They weren't even thinking about it. They were feeling." What is most revealing is that he adds, "Still, that was true of everybody. It was what you had to reckon with" (18 *Am V*). In the same book Marie Hasluck may think that she has freely decided to become first an anarchist, and then a literal believer in the power of love to overcome spears. In fact, the story makes it quite clear that her decisions are very much controlled by the situations in which she finds herself and are shaped by the cast of her mind as an "inner light mystic." [62] Nevertheless her decisions are hers and it is her faithfulness to her own nature that accounts for the partial judgment of her at the end as living on a level of heroism, in spite of being obviously and desperately wrong and narrow-minded.

Cary goes further; a major portion of his concern with children is to show to what extent personality is the result of external circumstances. Tabitha Bonser's son John seems to serve as an example of the failure of excessive permissiveness. He becomes an intellectual incapable of forceful action apparently largely due to the fact that his mother brought him up by bribing him with love rather than by use of strict rules, and also because she refused to let her creative husband, James Gollan, give him the meaningful expansion of spirit he was ready for as a child, but sent him instead to schools where his intellect, not his enthusiasm, was expanded. On the other hand, Philip Feenix becomes a suicide because his excessively permissive father and his overwhelming uncle between them have allowed him no life of his own. Nina's son, Tom, is another example of a person with the same problem.

On the other hand, freedom is possible under all circumstances. Musa, the young boy of *The African Witch*, is free both in his ability to face the new and in his way of life, which most of the time he spends in neither the Mohammedan nor pagan areas of town but rather in the wasteland between. He is an example of a free person who has become lost, in an objective sense, in a life which offers him neither the scope nor the education he could do so much with. Very similar to Musa is Charley, the main character of *Charley Is My Darling*, whose strong personal freedom makes him a dynamic and valued character, but also leads him into what society judges to be a life of crime and shame and for which it sends him to prison. In one sense the book is a study of childhood, for it shows the evil which improper education can do; at the same time the book attempts to explain how a child who is by nature creative and responsive can become criminal. Like Johnson, Charley goes bad as a result of the same elements of his personality which are his strengths. Like Johnson, he is sensitive, courageous, and imaginative, and he gets more pleasure from giving than from taking; like Johnson, his stealing is not in order to have money but rather to be the center of his followers, and he is pushed to excesses by his followers. Like Johnson, also, he responds not intellectually but with his total personality to the demands of his nature and is in this sense responsible for making himself a full human being.

Gulley Jimson is the most intellectual of all the free characters in Cary, but even in his case his intellect as such is largely related to his art. In other areas his decisions are made by the needs of his total personality, as for instance when he calls on the telephone, when he steals the Netsukes, and even when he moves into the Beeders' home. Wilcher too, though he pretends to act rationally, in fact acts by the compulsion of his personality as when he exposes himself, burns down his house, and causes himself to have a heart attack. It is not strange that these actions seem as much a necessary part of his free self as his acceptance of life and the need for change (which is typified by the hymn which gives its name to his book); they are as much a part of his freedom as Gulley's stealing and lying are an integral part of his creative personality. Gulley and Wilcher both become free men eventually because they both realize their own natures. If Gulley does so more than Wilcher, that advantage might perhaps be offset by his ability to kill. Plant and the people around him, on the other hand, are not free, because following their intellects excessively, they are caught up in their realization of the injustice of the world. This injustice certainly exists; Gulley and Wilcher get their comparative strength not from ignoring it, but rather from placing their commitment on the freedom which is its other dimension.

Throughout his work Cary always assumes that men are responsible for what they do and are. However, at the same time he never assumes that anyone can simply make himself do, or become, something which is foreign to what he already is at the time; there is a fatalism in all of Cary which is expressed by Rose's forgiveness of her sister Ella: "What is there to forgive? You are you and I am I, we are past changing" (105 *Moonlight*). This dichotomy adds another complication to the question of what freedom is. In fact the question of freedom is shot through with paradoxes. How can a man be following his duty if the concept of duty is self developed? How can a man be said to offer liberty to another when merely by offering he is limiting the other's response? How can a man be selfless when he is getting satisfaction from the selflessness? What are the moral limitations of freedom?

Such questions get their fullest treatment in the second trilogy, which as a result is the work with the most intense moral focus. In this trilogy, Chester Nimmo's point of departure is the sense of love and freedom, the underlying spiritual forces of reality, while Nina's is psychological; she observes and describes the mechanics by which Chester gets his sense of power. Jim Latter's is moral; he measures behavior by reference to what he takes to be an unchanging code.[63]

In a fundamental sense, the trilogy is a study of failure. At its end the two major characters have both shown their principles of life to be insufficient to sustain them. In most of the previous works the central characters were sinners whose story both explains and redeems them. Even Wilcher is redeemed by his final acceptance of life. However, Jim Latter, a man who thinks he lives by facts—truth and honor—kills the woman he loves for these very principles. Chester Nimmo thinks he is a man who lives by the twin principles of love and freedom, but brutally thrusts himself on the woman who is now married to another. The man of honor dies deservedly on the gallows. The man who proclaimed the sanctity of family affection dies in the W.C. after having been surprised by a jealous husband. Nina dies as she lived, but only because she is as she has always been, a victim, her throat cut by a madman she loves and whom she forgives.

There can be no question that Jim Latter comes off worst. Although he accuses Nimmo of hypocrisy it is he who saves his career as a soldier by running out on the cousin whom he has got pregnant. He has also made her pregnant twice after, while she was married to Nimmo, once when he was a guest in Nimmo's house. This is an element of the truth which he never mentions in his search for the facts. Nevertheless he feels free to include in the list of Nimmo's sins, the accusation that he destroyed the "sanctity of the home and marriage . . ." (9 *NHM*). Less personally, his insight into the historical and sociological situation is deficient, as his connection to the Lugas proves. He feels about this African tribe which was in his charge during his African exile exactly as Marie and all the other mistaken whites feel about the Africans in the earlier African books: "They were truly nature's gentlemen and the finest I ever knew. But since then entirely ruined and destroyed as a people by European so-called progress" (8 *NHM*). Chester on the other hand sees the issue in proper perspective. "I wonder if he is a good judge of what will help the natives?" he asks. "I know he's done some good work, but hasn't he been rather out of the stream all these years—things have moved since he went to Africa and they're moving even faster now. . . . We can't stop history in full course. And history is going all against the primitive—it always did. Jim should face the situation as it is" (283–84 *P of G*). Politically his views are equally wrong. Although Jim is essentially a nonpolitical figure—Nina points out in one of the letters which cause so much of a turmoil within Jim, "he was a political idiot" (215 *P of G*)—yet he has attitudes with political consequences, and his attitudes are essentially fascist. Although it is true that he wants nothing to do with Major Brightman, leader of a fascist group who tries to use Latter, it is just as true that he rejects him not because of his ideas but because of his personality. "The book [in which Brightman explains his presumably fascist version of "True Democracy"] was all right but I didn't much take to the fellow who smelt of brass. Also push" (38 *NHM*). Here again Nimmo's violent hatred for Brightman is the more proper one, even though Nimmo's hatred is also not entirely political. Curiously, Nimmo's violence towards Brightman sounds very much like Jim's toward Nimmo:

> I called you a Fascist . . . and so you are—your politics are on a par with your character. You are out for yourself by any dirty trick, any mean deceit by which you can take advantage of the misery of the poor for your own benefit and glory (55 *NHM*).

When Jim kills Nina he is in a sense acting out the furthest reach of his improper politics. Insane as the act is, he still thinks of it as a political act, explaining that she had to die, "Because of the grabbers and tapeworms who were sucking the soul out of England" (220 *NHM*).

Although Jim's views lead him to murder, Bloom has argued that Jim is not mad and that those who think he is "are not sensitive to the provocation to which Cary exposes Jim, and that consequently they are disposed to misconstrue exasperation and outrage as madness." [64] He insists also that Jim's insistence on honor, truth, and justice make him an attractive figure whose integrity is "perhaps the most meaningful kind of heroism possible in a backsliding, slipshod time," while of Jim's political incapacity he says that it is "by such stubborn repudiations of duplicity, expediency and corruption, that we are able to maintain our self-respect as men." [65] He further applauds Jim's denial of his madness—"They think me mad because I couldn't live like a rat," Jim says (223 *NHM*)—as an assertion of human dignity and personal integrity. The most Bloom is willing to admit is that it is possible to see Jim "as a crank, a man whatever his loyalties and integrity, quite unfit to live in the twentieth century." [66] Cary himself refuses to accept any such evaluation of Jim Latter. Politically he sides with Nimmo, as he made clear in a letter to Andrew Wright: "What I believe is what Nimmo believes, that wangle is inevitable in the modern state, that is to say, there is no choice between persuading people and shooting them." [67] In a handwritten notation quoted by Hoffman, Cary also makes it clear that he does not share Bloom's high evaluation of Jim's honor: "Jim's honour. Point out only artificial. Highest honour to sacrifice oneself. Afraid of public opinion—of what people will say. This 'honour' is artificial, trivial, it is *really cowardice*." [68]

Cary's comments quite aside, however, it is perfectly clear that Jim is a terrible failure by any acceptable standards. Certainly it is mad for a man to kill the woman he loves "for an example because it was necessary" (222 *NHM*), with the hopes of having the nation's corruption in this way exposed to public view.[69] No amount of talk of truth and honor can excuse such an action. Cary makes Jim's position as strong as he can and he explains him with great sympathy, but Cary is entitled to assume that every reader will know for himself that anyone who uses murder as a way out is insane. Furthermore, the truth is that his stated reason for the murder is at most only one portion of the full reason. Jim is a violent man, and has been one since childhood when he repeatedly grew furious with Nina. He is impatient with rules and law, although he pretends to respect them. "What is the good of your precious laws," he asks a lawyer, "if they can't distinguish between an honest man and the biggest known liars playing the dirtiest kind of political racket ever seen anywhere?" (152 *NHM*). He does not know himself very well, or he is lying, when he says that his discoveries of Nimmo and his wife were accidental. In one such case he announces that he will not be back before seven but returns at six, enters the house through the back door, "by pure chance" (7 *NHM*), and looks, by chance again, through the drawing room windows. Another time he leaves his car at the top of the lane, comes in through the kitchen garden, and makes directly for the bedroom (161 *NHM*). Obviously he was seeking the opportunity. When the moment finally presents itself Jim pretends to be cool, dispassionate, and involved in executing an act of justice. Clearly, however, this is not the case.

He claims that Nina deserves to die because of her part in the trial which has sent Maufe, one of Jim's own men in the Specials, to jail. Maufe has been accused of using excessive violence in arresting a communist leader, Pincombe, at Jim's orders, while Jim insists that Maufe simply did his duty. The court finds that he used excessive violence, partly because of Nina's evidence in the case. Without saying anything about the event of the arrest itself, Nina avoids answering questions referring to Nimmo's part in the affair. After Maufe is convicted, however, Jim discovers that Nina did have knowledge of the case, and that in fact she has acted as a go-between for Nimmo in several incidents related to the events, and that

Nimmo wanted Maufe convicted partly because it would increase his political chances.

However, the facts are still far from evident, and it would be quite false to assume that Jim has learned through the letters that Maufe was not guilty. The central question—whether the man used excessive violence or not—is not at all resolved through the letters between Nina and Nimmo.[70] When he kills Nina it is certainly not because he has a right to be convinced that she has sent an innocent man to prison. Maufe may have been innocent, or he may not have been; Jim is no more sure when he kills her than before. On the contrary, he is unsure of events, just as he is unsure of himself. Incapable of granting freedom, incapable of living in doubt, faced with a world which is less simple than he thinks it is, faced indeed with a reality which does not permit simple meanings to be given to the terms—honor, truth, justice —he turns to violence in much the same way as Rackham who in *The African Witch* assaults Aladai. It is an admission that his way of looking at reality has not been strong enough to stand the pressure of events.

Nimmo is a failure too, but not the same kind as Jim. He fails not because his vision of reality is insufficient, but rather because he cannot remain true to it. Chester Nimmo is the center of the trilogy and each of the books focuses on him. In the first trilogy a similar kind of central character is lacking. As Chester tells his own story he explains his fundamental vision of life, a vision which is rooted in the kind of love and devotion found in a large, hardworking family. Repeatedly, he fails to follow his vision of truth according to his own account. This occurs for instance in his acceptance of the falseness and lies of the union movement led by the communist, Pring—a failure paralleling the labor difficulties which Jim details in his book, where Nimmo again takes up common cause with a communist. He fails too in his inability to understand and return the love of his sister Georgina, a failure which parallels the unstable relationship to Nina which is described in her book. As Nina tells Chester's story, she explains the psychological devices by which Nimmo reaches his strength and she raises the question of Nimmo's sincerity. She recognizes that Nimmo is fanatical in his freedom and that he believes fully in a necessary personal relationship between man and God. She notices how prayer inspires him while at the same time he uses it as a source of inspiration. Similarly, she notices that Chester has the power to create his own excitement and keep up with it. Even in his personal relationships Chester mixes sincere belief and personal advantage. For instance when he grants to Nina and Jim the freedom which Jim is never willing to grant to Nina and Chester, perhaps because Jim took advantage of the freedom when he had the chance, Chester does so, she believes, not only because he believes in freedom but also because he feels it might be the right tactic in order to keep her bound to him and to prevent Jim from taking her away. In none of these cases does she actually accuse him of insincerity; nor does she do so as she gets to know him better, despite shifts in his political positions. Early in their relationship she is convinced that he is merely using the most available means to political success and ignoring truth and decency. Thus she is extremely upset when he attacks the landlords, including her relatives and friends, early in their marriage, and she thinks of the attack as consciously false. She gradually realizes, however, that he is sincere in the way he views the class structure—a structure which he thinks helps keep the poor poor. She accepts also his shift from pacifism before the First World War, which allows him to accept a cabinet post in a war government.[71] In each of these cases, as throughout his career, it is impossible to disentangle the sincere from the self-centered, impossible to determine where the man makes use of the spirit and where the spirit makes use of man.[72] But she does not blame him for this; unlike Jim she considers spirit a necessary element in any man who assumes responsibility and refuses a pale and cloistered virtue. She also sees Chester's role as necessary. As she says, in implicit criticism of Jim,

. . . no one has a *right* to hate Chester. After all, people who say they don't want much from life—only ordinary peace and

quiet—are really asking . . . a great deal. For the ordinary
thing is more like a violent argument about the right road
in a runaway coach galloping downhill in a fog. If no one
drives (and that means *choosing* a way) everything will crash
(262–63 *P of G*).

Of course, Chester fails by her standards of sincerity too, especially when he forsakes his oldest friend, Goold, and when
he threatens through an intermediary to have Jim put into
danger. Throughout, though, in spite of temporary abbera-
tions, she sees him as a fundamentally decent man trying to
do what he conceives of as good. At the same time, it is also
quite clear that she sees his final madness as having developed
straight from the peculiar tensions and provocations of his
life. His selfishness and devotion to his ideals, so long held
together, have finally split completely as he talks with the
assurance of an older statesman and with the conviction of
a preacher, while at the same time pawing her when no one
is looking. She sees him as she would a creature who, "from
sheer egotism or disease or age, has forgotten ordinary restraints and is so far mad" (371 *P of G*). [73] Nimmo deals with
the problems of remaining true to the spiritual reality which
reaches man through his intuition, and Nina deals with the
problems of sincerity as man tries to follow his vision. Jim
Latter brings up the problems which arise as man tries to
apply his vision to the actual situation, and as it affects other
men. Ironically it is Jim, the man who thinks of himself as
nonpolitical, who brings up the issues which are usually considered political. [74] Nina may reveal some details of the technique of getting elected and of using political sense, especially
in private life. But it is Jim who shows Chester's politics in
action as Chester thrusts himself into the middle of a strike,
gains control of an important committee, and finally tries to
use it as a stepping stone to get back to power. It is also
Jim's book which suggests that Nimmo is thinking largely in
terms of his handling of the crisis, that is not only how it
will affect his own career, but also how it will affect the party,
and the country as a whole. This is only one of the various

dimensions of Nimmo which Jim sees but does not understand.

Yet the moral questions which Jim introduces into the examination of Nimmo, like the questions of personal sincerity introduced by Nina, and the questions of the nature of intuition which Nimmo introduces about himself, are all valid ones. Each character introduces a valid standard of judgment —indeed a necessary standard. As a matter of fact it is a major purpose of the trilogy to show the complex nature of the Nimmo type of politician, and to make an honest attempt to come to grips with the problem of how to evaluate him.

In an article published shortly after the last volume of the trilogy was published, Cary makes it clear that his own standards of evaluating politicians are those used in the trilogy by all three of the narrators—sincerity, unselfishness, devotion to principle, and honesty.[75] He begins by refusing to accept the notion that politicians live in a world which is by its nature immoral, just as he refuses to accept the notion that politicians have a special right to lie because great issues are involved. "In fact," Cary says, "there is no double standard. Lies are always lies, evil is always evil. . . ."[76] On the other hand, by drawing an analogy with the mother who manages a family by properly evading the truth, Cary argues that the individual lie is less significant in making a full judgment than the total situation. The only ultimate standard, he says, is that of personal integrity. Of good politicians we want to know that

> . . . if they have broken a promise it was because they could not help it; if they did conceal some facts from us it was not for their good but ours. That in the final resort they have given their lives to serve what they conceive to be a good end; that they are not in politics for their own advantage or glory.[77]

To make a final appraisal of a politician, "we should ask what problems he faced . . . what kind of support he got, what pressure he withstood, what risks he took. But our final question will be still, 'Was he an honest man?' "[78]

The trilogy, complex as it is, shows a working out of this fundamental question. And by all of the standards used Nimmo comes off better than his rival who judges him and examines him; he has dared more, his vision is fuller, and on the whole he tried to be a good man. This is a major reason why Nina stays with him. Another reason is the tension which surrounds Chester and which draws her so strongly to him that she even forgets her own sympathies for the sake of Chester's campaigns.[79]

But the main reason she stays with him is that in offering her the freedom to choose, he also forces her to think of life in terms of duty. Her decision—or lack of decision—to stay with Nimmo is indeed at the core of the novel. Cary made this plain when he said that the railroad scene in which she chooses freely to return to Nimmo even though at this time she is perfectly free to leave was the trial balloon, and was written first. Once that scene worked out he knew the book could be done.[80] The whole point of the railroad scene is that she is unable to decide not to return to Nimmo, simply because he has made her see that her choice is not between two men, or between honesty and hypocrisy, but rather between a life of personal desires and a life of meaningful duty (88 *P of G*).

She becomes a victim of two men who need her because in large part each needs to dominate her. Jim wants to assert himself physically, in the traditional virile way. Chester wants to assert himself by controlling her feelings and emotions. Both speak of love but give up her love for her body. Jim leaves her for the sake of his career, coming back only occasionally for sex. Eventually Nimmo is satisfied to have her act as if she enjoyed sleeping with him. In a sense she is a mechanical aid to both men, even when they feel themselves closest to her. Ironically she makes Chester fall "into a real passion of love" (115 *P of G*) when she is anxious to get rid of Chester and so satisfies him with that sexual technique which Jim had learned in India and had taught her. In very much the same way she is able to comfort Jim at a critical moment for him because she had learned "from the last ten years' experience with Chester what my function was" (359

*P of G*). Both men wind up collaborating in her destruction. Both men, too, wind up without the fruit of marriage—Jim has children but cannot admit to them; Chester admits to children but hasn't fathered any.[81]

Nina is murdered. Her two husbands and lovers each become mad in their own way before they die—one in a bathroom, the other on the gallows. And yet the trilogy is a positive work in the sense that it affirms important fundamental values. Each of the books uses the same basic standards by which to measure men, decency, truth, sincerity, though the standards are applied in different ways. The man who most tries to live by these standards and who, though ultimately unsuccessful, comes closest to doing it is also the man who has greatest freedom of the mind, and who in addition is the man whose intuition has brought him closest to the spiritual reality. By these standards Chester Nimmo is not an extremely good man. But under the circumstances, he is perhaps the best man possible. He is certainly the freest.

# *Notes*

[1] See, for instance, "The Novelist At Work: A Conversation Between Joyce Cary and Lord David Cecil," *Adam International Review*, XVIII (November–December 1950), 24.

[2] *Case*, p. 12.

[3] *Ibid.*, p. 130.

[4] *Power in Men*, p. 53.

[5] *Ibid.*, pp. 116–17.

[6] *Art and Reality*, p. 138.

[7] "The Way A Novel Gets Written," *Harper's Magazine*, CC (February 1950), pp. 92–93. There is a confusion in terminology in Cary about this and other words. Sometimes "real" is meant to refer to everything that motivates individual men; sometimes it refers to all that is outside of men; sometimes it refers to the motivations of man which truly correspond to his basic nature and the reality outside of him. Cary is not especially consistent about matters of this sort. In a similar way he misuses his own terms, "freedom" and "liberty." In a 1954 article he carefully distinguishes between "freedom" (liberté personelle) and "liberty" ("le concept juridique

des droits"). "Notes sur l'art et la liberté," *Preuves*, XLII (August, 1954), 28–32. This usage is one he also seems to follow throughout *Power in Men*, but he nevertheless speaks there of liberty as "creation in the act," apparently referring not to a "concept juridique des droits," but rather to "liberté personelle." *Power*, p. 7.

8 *Power in Men*, p. 216.

9 *Art and Reality*, p. 5.

10 *Ibid.*, p. 28.

11 *Ibid.*, p. 29; my italics. Cary says "appears," not in order to throw doubt on the fact of the intuition, but rather because the gap bridged by intuition is not really that between the individual and reality; rather it is between the individual mind "and the universal consistencies of nature human and material as recorded by his sensibility." *Art and Reality*, p. 29. And by "sensibility" Cary means the total quality of mind of the individual as qualified by his education, his feelings, his knowledge, in fact all his experiences. See *ibid.*, p. 38.

12 This "objective" reality is in the long run no more objective than man's "subjective" reality. It exists in the mind of God, whom Cary sees as a personal being "existing in all space-time." *Power in Men*, p. 262. Cary thus sees nature as having a purpose *"which is always trying to emerge."* *Ibid.*, p. 261; Cary's italics. As for the obvious and not very fair question arising from any system which includes a purely subjective epistemology—how can any one who says that reality is different for each individual talk of reality at all?—Cary brushes it aside by stating, perhaps partly with tongue in cheek, that he does not intend his version of the truth to be taken as the absolute truth, for "no one can know what that is." *Art and Reality*, p. 13.

13 *Art and Reality*, p. 6.

14 Apparently Cary did not mean at all to suggest the book which used the title first, Goethe's *Dichtung und Wahrheit*.

15 *Case*, p. 73.

16 *Ibid.*, p. 11.

17 *Power in Men*, p. 192.

18 *Art and Reality*, pp. 5–6.

19 *Ibid.*, p. 148.

20 *Paris Review* interview, p. 67. Apparently Cary does not accept the negatives of these feelings as fundamental, and he nowhere speaks of hate, or an appreciation of ugliness as human nature. In this he is consistent with his belief that evil is the creation of man not God. See *Power in Men*, pp. 263–64. He would argue that human nature is the work of God, so that the existence of feelings like love is in itself a proof of the existence of God.

21 *Power in Men*, p. 76.

22 *Ibid.*, p. 77.

23 *Ibid.*, pp. 80–87.

[24] *Case*, p. 27. Political freedom here should not be confused with current usage as synonymous with national independence. While nationalism was a major concern in *The African Witch*, in general national independence for African states was not a live issue for Cary.

[25] For a general discussion of the major definitions of liberty see Isaiah Berlin, *Two Concepts of Liberty* (Oxford: Oxford University Press, 1958).

[26] *Power in Men*, p. 3.

[27] *Art and Reality*, p. 44.

[28] *The Process of Real Freedom* (London: Michael Joseph, 1943).

[29] *Power in Men*, pp. 11–12.

[30] "Proposals for Peace—III," *Nation*, CLXXVI (January 10, 1953), 28.

[31] "The Idea of Progress," *Cornhill*, 331. There is an element of the propagandist in all of Cary. He asserts that what is desirable is also what is inevitable, just as politicians regularly predict their victories. To insist with so little qualification that there is progress in our century of destruction may be such propaganda, or it may be naïve, or it may be whistling in the dark.

[32] "Joyce Cary's Last Look at His Worlds," *Vogue* (August 15, 1957), 153.

[33] "The Front-Line Feeling," *Listener* (January 17, 1952), 93.

[34] See esp. "Joyce Cary's Last Look" and "The Revolution of the Women," *Vogue* (March 15, 1951), 99, 100, 149.

[35] "My First Novel," *Listener* (April 16, 1953), p. 638.

[36] *Case*, p. 131.

[37] *Ibid.*, p. 34.

[38] *Power*, pp. 62–63.

[39] *Ibid.*, p. 48. For the full discussion see the entire chapter, "Man and State: Which is Master," pp. 32–63.

[40] *Ibid.*, p. 87.

[41] *Case*, p. 24. "Real" here means relating to specific individuals.

[42] *Power*, p. 14.

[43] *Ibid.*, p. 252. "Liberty" here apparently is not political but personal freedom.

[44] *Case*, p. 111.

[45] *Power*, p. 15.

[46] *Ibid.*, pp. 69–70.

[47] *Ibid.*, p. 14.

[48] *Power*, p. 152.

[49] *Art and Reality*, p. 146.

[50] *Power*, p. 169.

[51] *Ibid.*, p. 252.

52 *Ibid.*, p. 254.

53 *Ibid.*, p. 255.

54 *Ibid.*, p. 256.

55 See, for instance, the interesting discussion of allegory in Chapters 32 to 35 of *Art and Reality;* "The Way a Novel Gets Written"; and "A Novelist and His Public," *Listener* (September 30, 1954), 521, 522.

56 *Art and Reality*, p. 112.

57 See Wright, *Joyce Cary*, p. 26.

58 *Mahood*, p. 110.

59 *Ibid.*, p. 119.

60 *Ibid.*, p. 123.

61 See also the discussion of Aissa's sacrifice above, pp. 59–63. It would not help the present discussion to pursue the interesting psychological aspects of Aissa's situation, or that of other characters like her who project parts of themselves into superpersonal demands. Such a discussion would enter into the actual way in which ethics operate; it would not help to define freedom.

62 The term is Cottee's but it is certainly trustworthy.

63 Since Cary has made it clear that he considers the moral sense an unstable guide, Jim's approach is not going to be an acceptable one. See *Power*, pp. 69–70.

64 *Indeterminate World*, pp. 193–94. All this exasperated outrage is evidently not enough to make Jim tell the facts as he knows them to Potter, an old friend who is being ruined by the strike (129–32 *NHM*). That would be breaking the rules. Yet the exasperation is supposed to be enough to cause him to commit murder.

65 *Ibid.*, p. 194.

66 *Ibid.*, p. 195.

67 Quoted in Wright, *Joyce Cary*, p. 154. Bloom mentions this letter but doesn't consider that it really applies to Jim's case. Jim, Bloom says, "does not desire to shoot people as a means of running the state, but merely to proceed in all things truthfully, justly, and honorably, if a little inflexibly," p. 197. The force of that final "a little inflexibly" will strike ordinary, less determinate readers than Bloom with some amazement.

68 Quoted in Hoffman, *Joyce Cary*, p. 155, Cary's italics.

69 When Jim is about to kill Nimmo he makes it clear that what he is after is publicity: "there's only one answer. You run your show on publicity for the mob and that's what I've got to do. To hit the headlines in a big way. To make an example" (219 *NHM*).

70 See also above, pp. 114–15.

71 Cf. For an interesting history and defense of nonconformists in British foreign affairs see A. J. P. Taylor, *The Trouble Makers: Dissent Over Foreign Policy, 1792–1932* (London: Hamish Hamilton, 1957). See esp. p. 21.

72 Nina's defense of Nimmo is completely rationalistic. She never accepts, for instance, as Cary himself would, that Nimmo's faith may have objective validity and that through his intuition he might well be in touch with the actual shape of reality, a connection which might in fact account for his spiritual strength.

73 At several points throughout the book he appears to her as removed from himself. Tom is able to imitate him because he can see him as not organically alive. She sees him as a puppet, literally (277 *P of G*), and in a related image, when he is in her arms, as, "a nasty little animal" (63 *P of G*).

74 Cary, it is obvious, refuses to limit the meaning of the word "political," and insists on using it to include all three approaches and more, the total context of human relations.

75 "Political and Personal Morality," *Saturday Review* (December 31, 1955), pp. 5–6, 31–32.

76 *Ibid.,* p. 6.

77 *Ibid.,* p. 31.

78 *Ibid.,* p. 32.

79 Since she is a divided woman it is not at all extraordinary that her own preference is for a life of peace and a lack of commitment. Her memory of delight as a child for instance, was to lie hidden and unseen while looking down into the world (143 *P of G*).

80 See *The Indeterminate World,* pp. 134–35.

81 Nina and Jim's son Robert, born to them during their marriage, plays no apparent role in the book at all.

# Bibliography

## 1. NOVELS BY JOYCE CARY

*The African Witch.* Carfax Edition, London: Michael Joseph, 1951.

*Aissa Saved.* Carfax Edition, London: Michael Joseph, 1952.

*An American Visitor.* Carfax Edition, London: Michael Joseph, 1952.

*The Captive and the Free.* New York: Harper and Row, 1959.

*Castle Corner.* Carfax Edition, London: Michael Joseph, 1952.

*Charley Is My Darling.* Carfax Edition, London: Michael Joseph, 1951.

*Except the Lord.* London: Michael Joseph, 1953.

*A Fearful Joy.* Carfax Edition, London: Michael Joseph, 1952.

*Herself Surprised.* Carfax Edition, London: Michael Joseph, 1951.

*The Horse's Mouth.* Carfax Edition, London: Michael Joseph, 1951.

*A House of Children.* Carfax Edition, London: Michael Joseph, 1951.

*Mister Johnson.* Carfax Edition, London: Michael Joseph, 1952.

*The Moonlight.* Carfax Edition, London: Michael Joseph, 1952.

*Not Honour More.* London: Michael Joseph, 1955.

*Prisoner of Grace.* Carfax Edition, London: Michael Joseph, 1954.

*To Be a Pilgrim.* Carfax Edition, London: Michael Joseph, 1951.

## 2. SHORT FICTION BY JOYCE CARY

"The Old Strife At Plant's," *Harper's Magazine*, CCI (1950), 80–96.

*Spring Song and Other Stories*. London: Michael Joseph, 1960.

## 3. NONFICTION BY JOYCE CARY

*Art and Reality*, New York: Harper and Row, 1958.

"The Art of Fiction VII: Joyce Cary," *Paris Review*, No. 7 (Fall-Winter 1954–1955), 63–78. Interview conducted by John Burrows and Alex Hamilton.

*The Case for African Freedom and Other Writings on Africa.* Austin: University of Texas Press, 1962.

"The Front-Line Feeling," *Listener* (Jan. 17, 1952), 92–93.

"The Idea of Progress," *Cornhill*, CLXVII (1954), 331–37.

"Joyce Cary's Last Look at His Worlds," *Vogue* (August 15, 1957), 96–97, 150–51, 153.

"My First Novel," *Listener* (April 16, 1955), 637–38.

"Notes sur l'art et la liberté," *Preuves*, No. 42 (August, 1954), 28–32.

"A Novelist and His Public," *Listener*, LII (September 30, 1954), 521–22.

"The Novelist at Work: A Conversation Between Joyce Cary and Lord David Cecil," *Adam International Review*, XVIII (November-December 1950), 15–25.

"Political and Personal Morality," *Saturday Review* (December 31, 1955), 5–6, 31–32.

*Power in Men.* Seattle: University of Washington Press, 1963.

*The Process of Real Freedom.* London: Michael Joseph, 1943.

"Proposals For Peace—III," *Nation* (January 10, 1953), 28.

"The Revolution of the Women," *Vogue* (March 15, 1951), 99, 100, 149.

"The Way a Novel Gets Written," *Harper's Magazine*, CC (February 1950), 87–93.

## 4. OTHER WORKS

Adams, Hazard. "Blake and Gulley Jimson: English Symbolists," *Critique*, III (1959), 3–14.

———. "Joyce Cary's Three Speakers," *Modern Fiction Studies*, V (1959), 108–20.

Alter, Robert. *Rogue's Progress: Studies in the Picaresque Novel.* Cambridge: Harvard University Press, 1964.

Auerbach, Erich. *Mimesis.* Garden City: Doubleday, 1957.

Bergson, Henri. *Laughter.* In *Comedy,* ed. Wylie Sypher. Garden City: Doubleday Anchor, 1956.

Berlin, Isaiah. *The Hedgehog and the Fox.* New York: Simon and Schuster, 1953.

————. *Two Concepts of Liberty.* Oxford: Oxford University Press, 1958.

Bettman, Elizabeth. "Joyce Cary and the Problem of Political Morality," *Antioch Review,* XVII (1957), 266–72.

Bloom, Robert. *The Indeterminate World: A Study of the Novels of Joyce Cary.* Philadelphia: University of Pennsylvania Press, 1962.

Booth, Wayne C. *The Rhetoric of Fiction,* Chicago: University of Chicago Press, 1961.

Burke, Kenneth. *Counter-statement.* Chicago: University of Chicago Press, 1957.

Case, Edward. "The Free World of Joyce Cary," *Modern Age,* III (1959), 115–24.

French, Warren G. "Joyce Cary's American Rover Girl," *Texas Studies in Literature and Language,* II (1960), 281–91.

Frye, Northrop. *Anatomy of Criticism: Four Essays.* Princeton: Princeton University Press, 1957.

Fyfe, Christopher. "The Colonial Situation in *Mister Johnson,*" *Modern Fiction Studies,* IX (1963), 226–30.

Garrett, George. "The Major Poetry of Joyce Cary," *Modern Fiction Studies,* IX (1963), 245–56.

Grant, Douglas. "The Novel and Its Critical Terms," *Essays in Criticism,* I (1951), 421–29.

Hall, James. *The Tragic Comedians: Seven Modern Masters.* Bloomington: Indiana University Press, 1963.

Hoffman, Charles G. "The Genesis and Development of Joyce Cary's First Trilogy," *PMLA,* LXXVIII (1963), 431–39.

————. *Joyce Cary: The Comedy of Freedom.* Pittsburgh: The University of Pittsburgh Press, 1964.

Kettle, Arnold. *An Introduction to the English Novel,* Vol. II. London: Hutchinson University Library, 1953.

Mahood, M. M. *Joyce Cary's Africa.* Boston: Houghton Mifflin, 1965.

Mitchell, Giles. "Joyce Cary's *Prisoner of Grace,*" *Modern Fiction Studies,* IX (1963), 263–75.

Schorer, Mark. "Fiction and the 'Matrix of Analogy,' " *Kenyon Review,* IX (1949), 539–60.

———. "The 'Socially Extensive' Novel," *Adam International Review,* XVIII (November-December, 1950), 31–32.

Stockholder, Fred. "The Triple Vision in Joyce Cary's First Trilogy," *Modern Fiction Studies,* IX (1963), 276–83.

Taylor, A. J. P. *The Trouble Makers: Dissent Over Foreign Policy, 1792–1932.* London: Hamish Hamilton, 1957.

Tindall, William York. *The Literary Symbol.* New York: Columbia University Press, 1955.

Tomkins, Calvin. "Beyond the Machine," *New Yorker,* XXXVII (February 10, 1962), 44–93.

Trilling, Lionel. *The Liberal Imagination.* New York: Doubleday Anchor, 1953.

Van Ghent, Dorothy. *The English Novel: Form and Function.* New York: Rinehart, 1953.

Weintraub, Stanley. *"Castle Corner,* Joyce Cary's *Buddenbrooks,"* Wisconsin Studies in Literature, V (1964), 54–63.

Wright, Andrew. *Joyce Cary: A Preface to His Novels.* New York: Harper, 1958.

# Index

main